88 Tips for Chromebook

2019 Edition

Kevin Wilson

88 Tips for Chromebook

Copyright © 2019 Elluminet Press

This work is subject to copyright. All rights are reserved by the Publisher, whether the whole or part of the material is concerned, specifically the rights of translation, reprinting, reuse of illustrations, recitation, broadcasting, reproduction on microfilms or in any other physical way, and transmission or information storage and retrieval, electronic adaptation, computer software, or by similar or dissimilar methodology now known or hereafter developed. Exempted from this legal reservation are brief excerpts in connection with reviews or scholarly analysis or material supplied specifically for the purpose of being entered and executed on a computer system, for exclusive use by the purchaser of the work. Duplication of this publication or parts thereof is permitted only under the provisions of the Copyright Law of the Publisher's location, in its current version, and permission for use must always be obtained from the Publisher. Permissions for use may be obtained through Rights Link at the Copyright Clearance Centre. Violations are liable to prosecution under the respective Copyright Law.

Trademarked names, logos, and images may appear in this book. Rather than use a trademark symbol with every occurrence of a trademarked name, logo, or image we use the names, logos, and images only in an editorial fashion and to the benefit of the trademark owner, with no intention of infringement of the trademark.

The use in this publication of trade names, trademarks, service marks, and similar terms, even if they are not identified as such, is not to be taken as an expression of opinion as to whether or not they are subject to proprietary rights.

Publisher: Elluminet Press

About the Author

With over 15 years' experience in the computer industry, Kevin Wilson has made a career out of technology and showing others how to use it. After earning a master's degree in computer science, software engineering, and multimedia systems, Kevin has held various positions in the IT industry including graphic & web design, building & managing corporate networks, training, and IT support.

He currently serves as Elluminet Press Ltd's senior writer and director, he periodically teaches computer science at college in South Africa and serves as an IT trainer in England. His books have become a valuable resource among the students in England, South Africa and our partners in the United States.

Kevin's motto is clear: "If you can't explain something simply, then you haven't understood it well enough." To that end, he has created the Exploring Technology Series, in which he breaks down complex technological subjects into smaller, easy-to-follow steps that students and ordinary computer users can put into practice.

Contents

Talk to your Chromebook 8
Using the Desktop 9
Find Settings & Preferences 10
One Finger Tap 11
Right Click 11
One Finger Click and Drag 12
Two Finger Scroll 12
Two Finger Swipe 13
Display All Open Apps 13
Find Keyboard Shortcuts 14
The Delete Key 15
Home and End Keys 16
Launching Apps 17
Pin Apps to your App Shelf 18
Create App Folders 19
Remove Apps 20
Task Manager 21
Cloud Enabled Printers 22
Connecting Older Printers 24
Adding Bluetooth Devices 26
Adding Other Users 28
Expand Storage with SD Card 30

- External Drives 31
- Quick Lock Your Screen 32
- Sign in as Guest 33
- Taking Screenshots 33
- Change Desktop Wallpaper 34
- Photo as Desktop Wallpaper 35
- Creating Documents 36
- Creating Spreadsheets 38
- Creating Presentations 40
- Using Google Drive 42
- Google Drive on Any Device 43
- Working Offline 45
- Transferring Files 46
- Bookmarking Websites 47
- Printing Webpages 49
- Pin Websites to your Shelf 50
- Reading Email 51
- Emailing Attachments 52
- Insert an Image 53
- Add Other Email Accounts 55
- Add Contact from Message 57
- Add Event to Calendar 58
- Call Someone on Hangouts 61
- Integrate DropBox 63

Integrate OneDrive	64
Remote Desktop	65
Reset with Powerwash	68
Keep Chromebook up to Date	69
Download Chrome Apps	70
Listen to Music	73
Streaming Music	76
Send Music to Other Device	77
Find your Favourite Movie	78
Watching Movies	81
Use ChromeCast	83
Watch TV Programs	84
Watch Youtube	85
Read a Book	86
Download More Books	87
Opening Photos	89
Add Filters to Photos	90
Enhancing Photos	90
Crop a Photo	92
Rotate Photos	93
Creating Photo Albums	94
Creating Photo Collages	96
Sharing Photos	97
Power Up	99

Power Off	99
Enable Android Apps	100
Install Android Apps	100
Minimise an App	102
Maximise an App	102
Flick Between Open Apps	103
Screen Brightness	103
Volume Control	103
Mute All	104
Autohide Shelf	104
Zoom into your Screen	105
Zoom out of your Screen	105
Reset Screen Zoom	105
Index	106

Talk to your Chromebook

The 'Google Now voice' assistant is integrated into Chromebook, but isn't always enabled by default.

To enable the feature, go to settings. Scroll down to 'Google Assistant'.

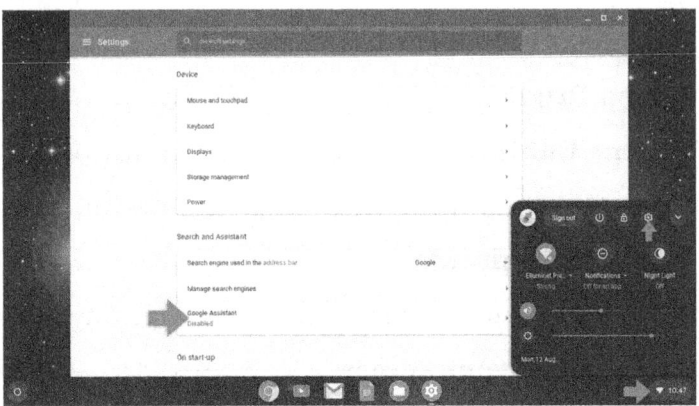

Turn on 'Google Assistant', also turn on 'Ok Google'.

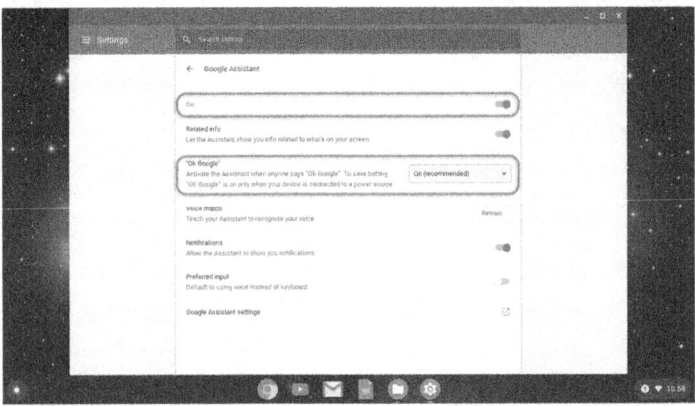

Go through the setup wizard to teach Google to recognise your voice.

Now, whenever you want something just say 'Hey Google...'

Using the Desktop

Along the bottom of your screen, you'll find a taskbar...

On the left hand side of the app shelf you have what looks like a magnifying glass icon. This is your App Launcher and allows you to open any app that has been added to your ChromeBook, as well as searching the web.

The next icon along is the Google Chrome web browser. This works just like any web browser you would find on a PC or Mac and allows you to search the web, use web apps, and use the internet how you would on any other computer.

The space on the app shelf after the Google Chrome icon can be for pinning any other app for quick access. For example, you could add, Google Photos, Gmail, Google Drive, word processing apps and so on.

On the right hand side of the app shelf you will find a few small icons.

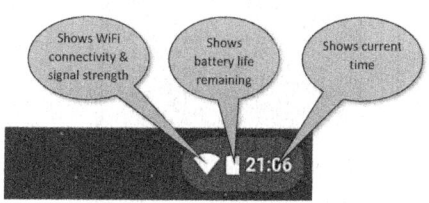

The first one along shows notifications such as new emails or system messages, reminders and so on. The next one across shows WiFi or ethernet connectivity. Next you have an icon for battery level, and the clock. Click on the icon to reveal the system tray.

Find Settings & Preferences

The system tray contains all your controls to connect to a WiFi network, pair a bluetooth device, change audio volume, screen brightness, sign in & out, or shut down. To reveal the system tray, click on the clock status icon on the bottom right of your screen.

Lets take a look at the various parts...

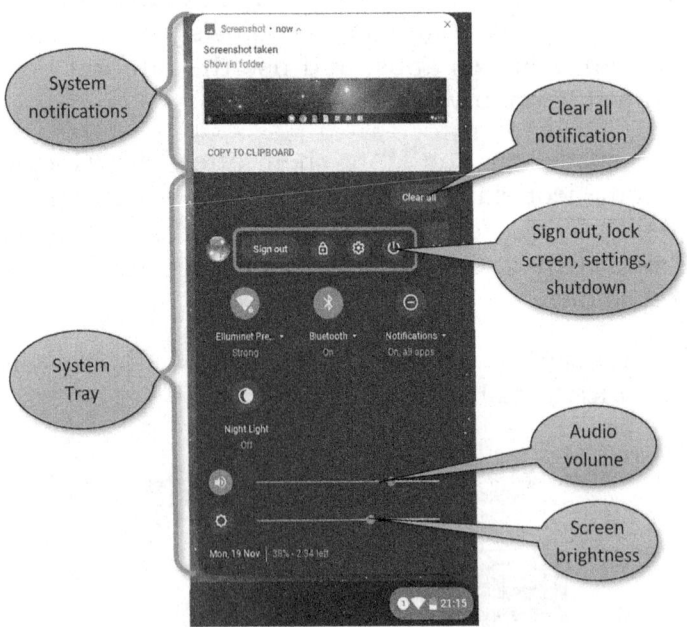

One Finger Tap

This is like your left mouse button and can be used to select objects such as icons or text fields on the screen. Just tap your finger on the pad.

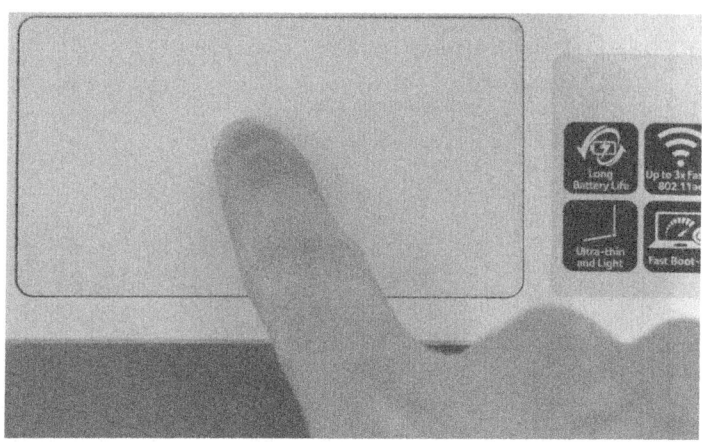

Right Click

This is like the right mouse button and can be used to right click on objects such as icons to reveal a context menu of options. Just tap both fingers on the pad at the same time.

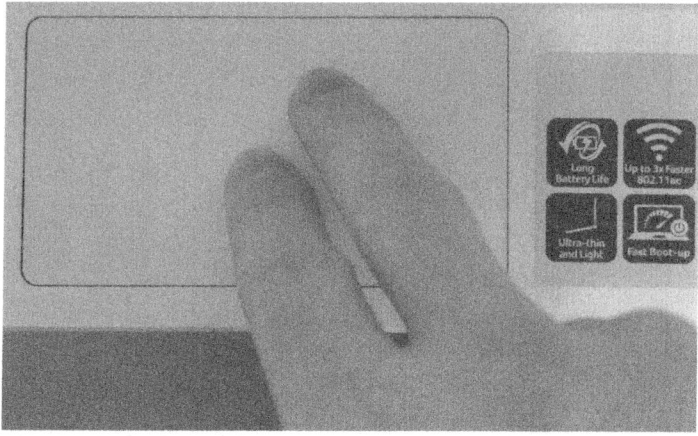

One Finger Click and Drag

Position your pointer on to an object such as window title bar, or image on your screen, then press your finger on the touch pad until you hear a click, then without releasing your finger, drag across the track pad to move the object.

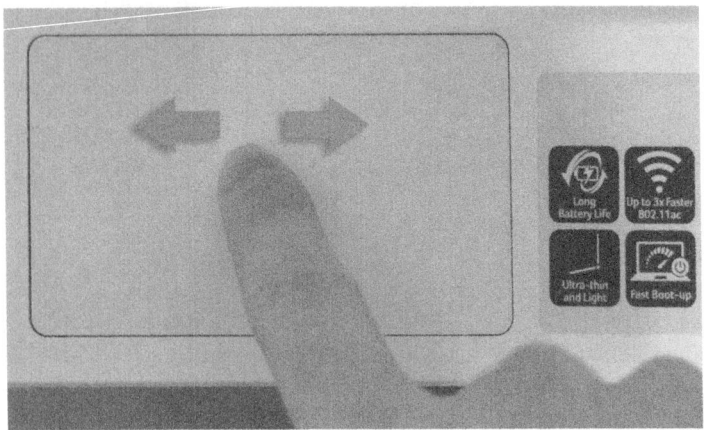

Two Finger Scroll

You can use two fingers on the track pad to scroll up and down windows, web pages, maps and so on.

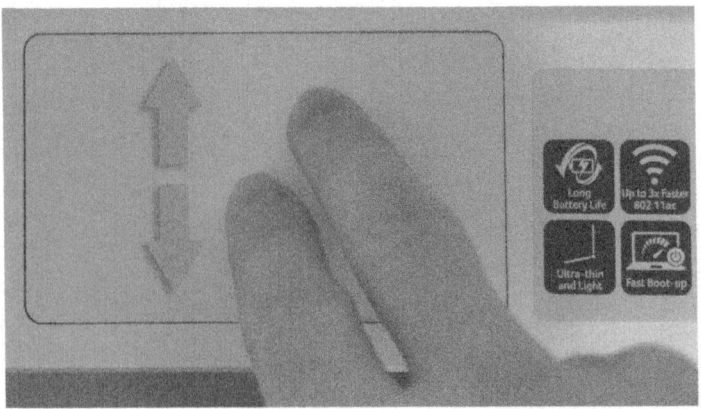

Two Finger Swipe

While you are browsing the web, you can go back to a previous page by swiping your two fingers to the left on the track pad and advance forward a page you have visited by swiping to the right.

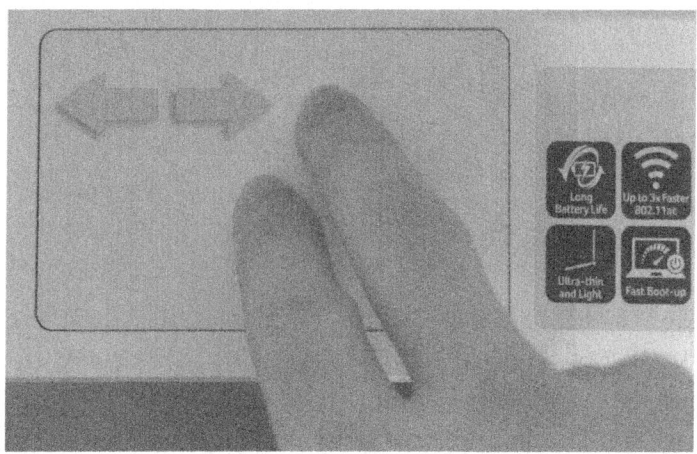

Display All Open Apps

You can quickly display all your open apps by swiping your three fingers downwards on the track pad.

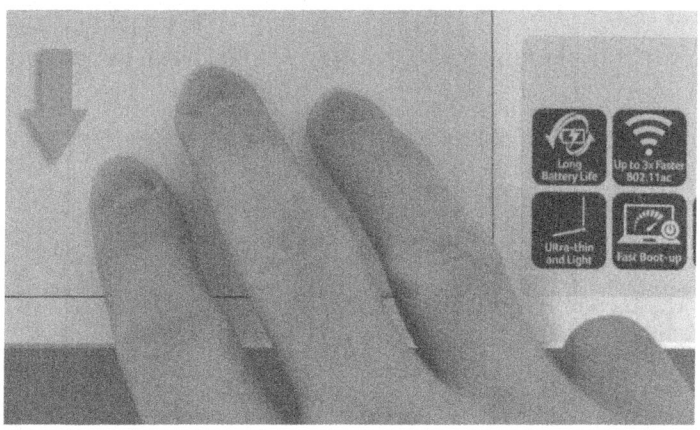

Find Keyboard Shortcuts

Chromebook has a help screen that shows you all the keyboard shortcuts available. Press **ctrl alt ?** to reveal the help screen.

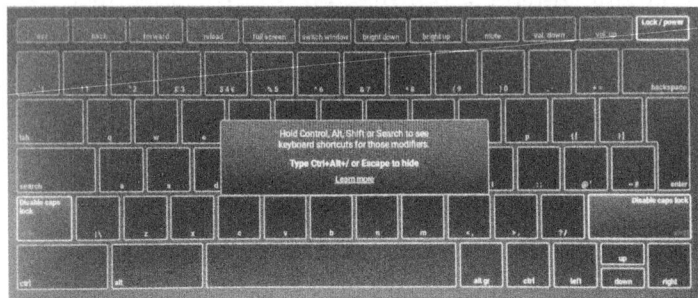

Now hold down the ctrl key and you'll see all the keyboard shortcuts highlighted on the keyboard.

You can also press alt or shift to see those keyboard shortcuts.

The Delete Key

There is no delete key in most Chromebook keyboards, however you can use a keyboard shortcut to do the same thing.

ALT Backspace to delete letter after cursor.

CTRL Backspace to delete word before cursor.

Home and End Keys

You can use the following keyboard shortcuts to jump to the beginning or end of a line of text.

CTRL ALT Up Arrow to jump to the beginning of a line

CTRL ALT Down Arrow to jump to the end of a line

Launching Apps

The App Launcher is very much like your start menu in Windows and is where you will find all the apps that have been installed on your ChromeBook.

To reveal the App Launcher, click the circle icon on the bottom left of your screen.

Click the arrow on the top middle of the launcher to open it up.

From here, you can search the web by entering a web site address or some keywords as you would normally do when using Google Search.

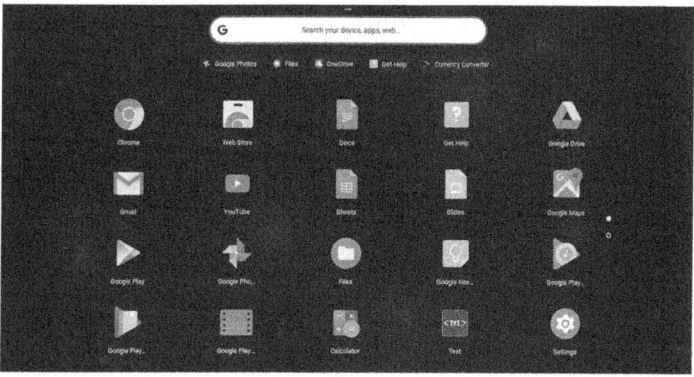

Below this, you'll see icons representing the apps installed on your ChromeBook.

Scroll up and down to see apps on the additional pages if required. Click on an icon to start the app.

Pin Apps to your App Shelf

The app shelf is similar to the task bar in Windows 10 and you can pin app icons to this shelf for quick access. So you can add all your most used apps to this shelf and click them when you need them.

To do this, open up your App Launcher and click the arrow at the top to reveal all the apps.

From this window, right click on the app icon you want to pin to your shelf.

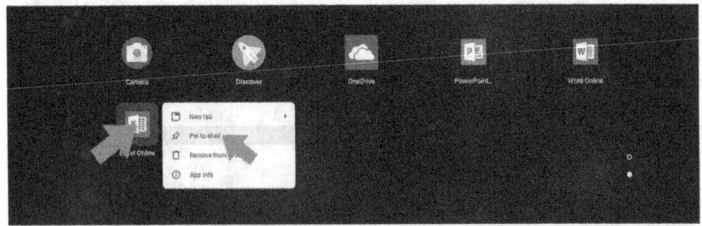

From the popup menu, click on 'pin to shelf'. You will see the app icon appear on the shelf at the bottom left of the screen, as shown below.

Create App Folders

You can group your apps into folders on your app launcher. The idea is to group apps that are of the same type. For example, you can group all your productivity apps together, eg Docs, Sheets, Slides.

To do this, just click and drag an icon on top of another.

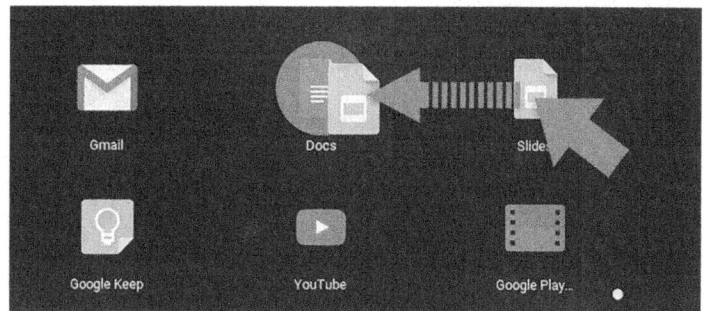

Click on the new folder to open it up.

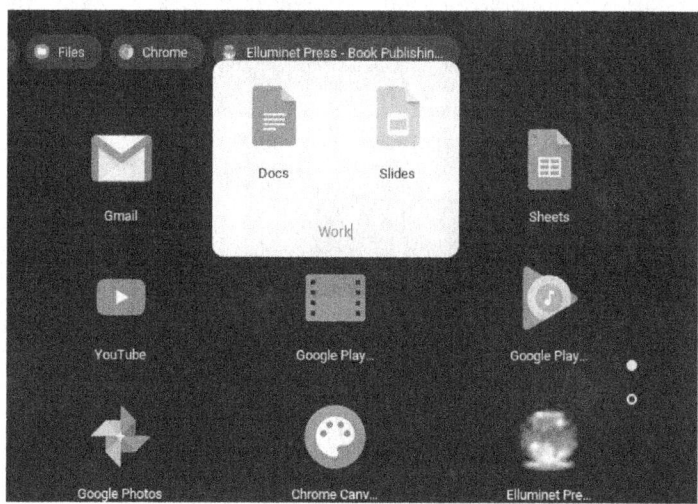

Click on the 'untitled' name at the bottom of the folder and type in something more meaningful.

Remove Apps

To remove an app, open your app launcher from the bottom left hand side of the screen. Click the arrow in the centre to reveal all your apps.

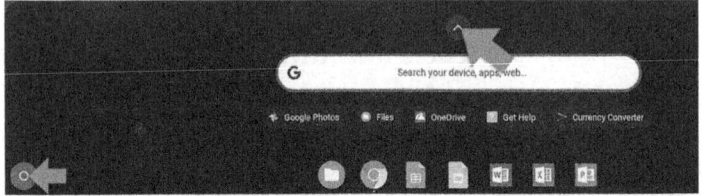

Right click on the app you want to remove.

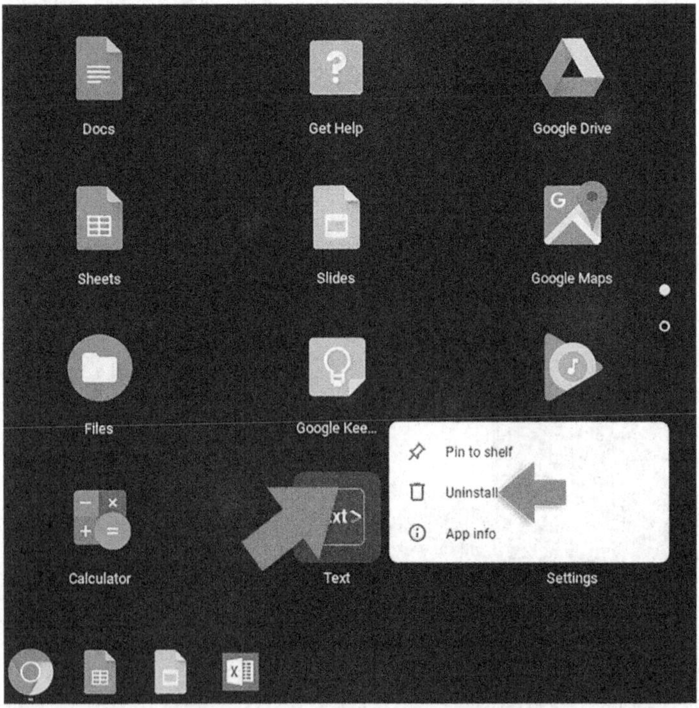

From the popup menu, click 'uninstall'.

Do this for all the apps you want to remove.

Task Manager

Hold down the **search** key, then tap **escape**. The search key looks like a small magnifying glass, you'll find it on the left hand side of your keyboard. On the old ChromeBooks press shift-escape.

You'll see a window pop up with a list of tasks (apps) that are currently running, as well as how much memory and cpu time they're using.

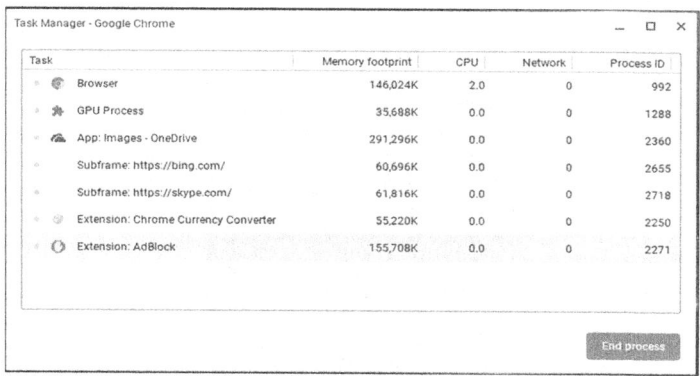

The task manager is useful if an app is not responding or has crashed.

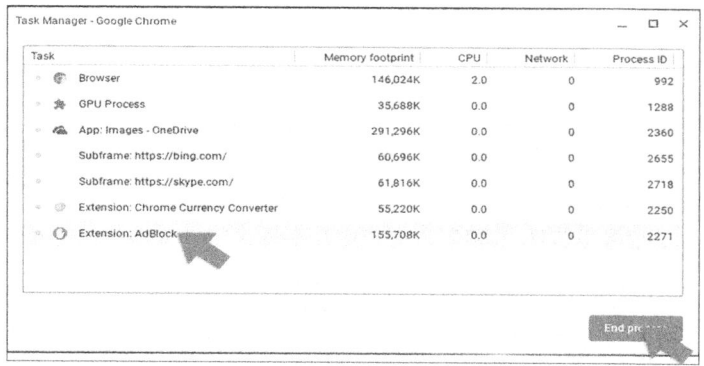

Just click on the task (app) in the list, then click 'end process'. The non-responsive app is usually labelled 'not responding'.

Cloud Enabled Printers

Your printer needs to support Google Cloud Print - you can check this in the documentation that came with your printer.

Turn on your printer and make sure it's connected to your WiFi.

On your ChromeBook, click the clock on the bottom right to open the system tray, then click the 'settings' icon.

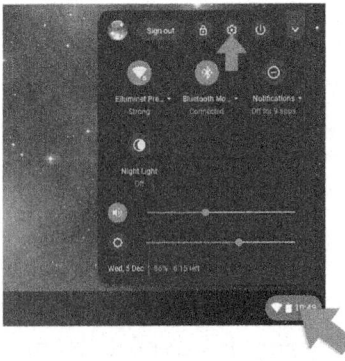

Scroll down to the bottom of the page and click 'advanced'.

Scroll down to the 'printing' settings, then click 'Google Cloud Print'.

Under the 'google cloud print' settings, click 'manage cloud print devices'.

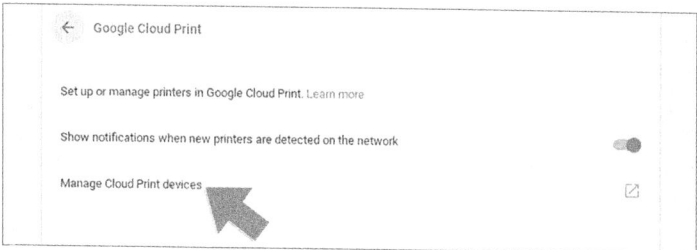

Your ChromeBook will scan for new devices. Any cloud enabled printers it finds will be listed under 'new devices'.

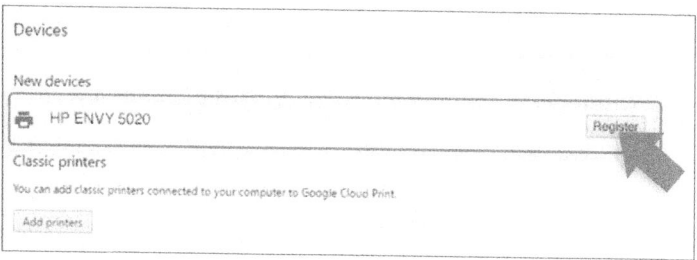

Click 'register' next to the printer's name.

It will take a few moments for your printer to be added. Once the setup is complete, you'll see your printer listed under 'my devices'.

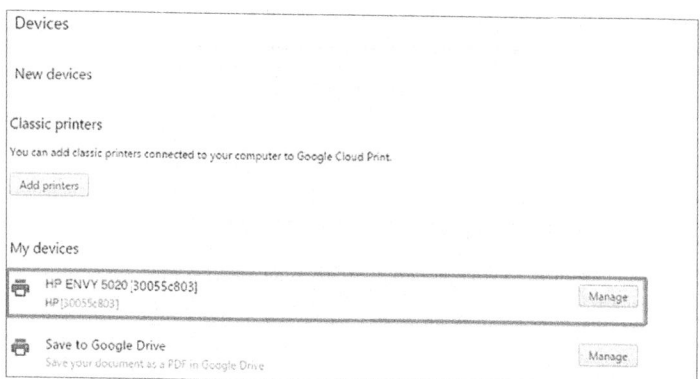

Connecting Older Printers

If your printer is a bit older and isn't cloud enabled, you can plug it into your ChromeBook using a USB cable. This is the simplest way to connect an older printer.

First, plug your printer into your ChromeBook using a USB cable.

On your ChromeBook, click the clock on the bottom right of your screen to open the system tray.

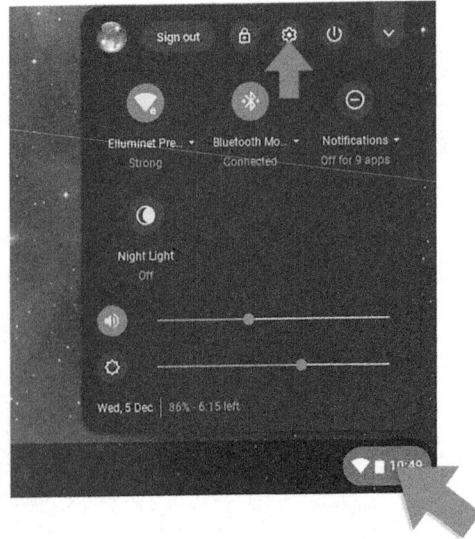

Then click the settings icon. Scroll down and click 'advanced'.

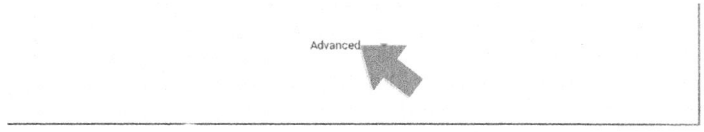

Scroll down to the 'printing' settings, then click 'printers'.

Click 'add printer'.

Click 'add nearby printers' on the bottom left of the dialog box.

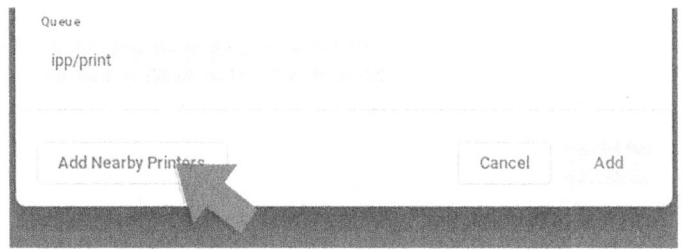

Your ChromeBook will scan for 'near by' printers, or printers that are plugged into your ChromeBook. This process can be a bit temperamental, especially with older printers, so you may need to refresh the settings screen using the refresh button on the top row of the keyboard.

Once detected, your printer will be listed. Click on it, then select 'add' on the bottom right.

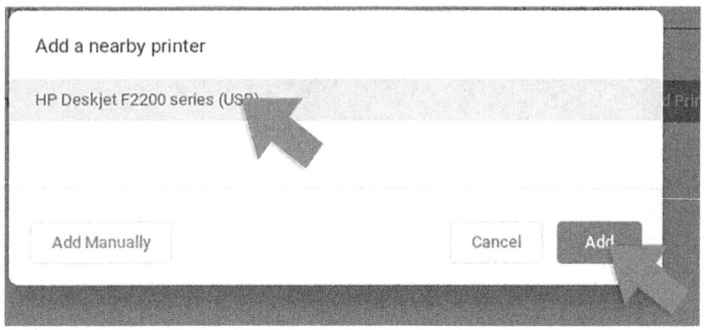

Adding Bluetooth Devices

You can add bluetooth mice, headphones, keyboards to your ChromeBook. This process is called pairing.

To add a bluetooth device, you need to put the device into pairing mode. To do this, press the pairing button on the bottom of the device - you might need to read the device's instructions on how to do this.

In this example, I'm going to add a bluetooth mouse. First power the mouse on and press the pairing button underneath. The light will begin to flash.

On your ChromeBook, click on the clock on the bottom right to open the system tray.

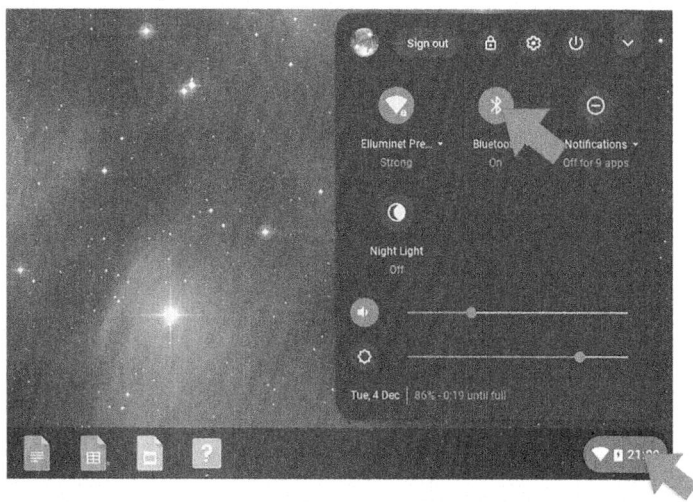

Select the bluetooth icon and turn it on if it isn't already.

Allow your ChromeBook to scan for nearby devices, this will take a minute or two. Once a device has been found, it will appear in the list.

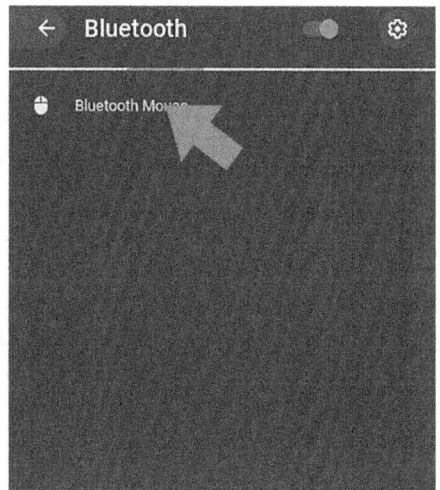

Click on the device in the list to connect it.

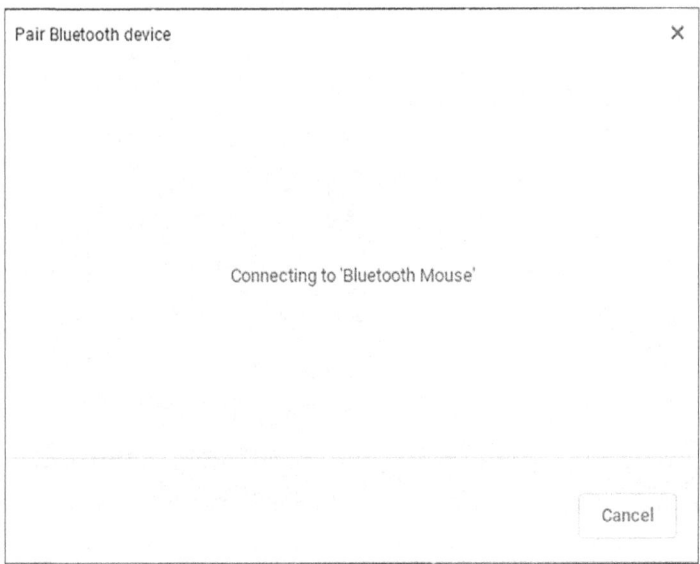

Once your ChromeBook has made a connection, you can use your device as normal.

Adding Other Users

You can add two types of users to your ChromeBook.

The first is a guest. This allows any user to get onto your ChromeBook without having to sign in with a Google Account. Guest users do *not* have access to the app store, Google+ or a Google email account, they can pretty much just browse the internet.

The other type, is a user with a Google Account. This is useful if more than one person uses your ChromeBook and need access to their own email, apps, and files. This is the recommended way to use your ChromeBook.

Users with a Google Account can access the full range of apps, use their email, Google+ and purchase apps from the App Store. Click 'add person' from the login screen.

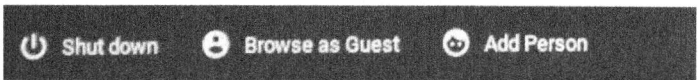

Allow them to sign in with their Google Account username and password.

Click 'next'.

Expand Storage with SD Card

Put an SD card into the card slot on the side of your Chromebook and you can use it just like local or Google Drive storage.

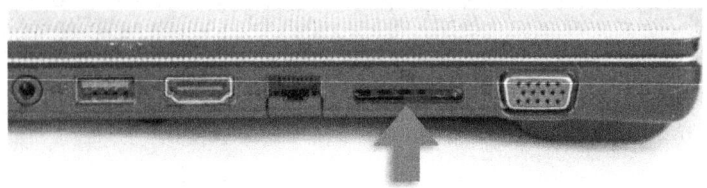

Open your files app. You'll find the icon on the app launcher.

The SD card will show up in the files app. Here, you can copy files onto the card.

To eject the card, click the eject icon. You can also format or rename the card. To do this, right click on the card in the files app.

External Drives

You can use a flash drive or external hard drive that has enough space to store your data.

Plug the external drive into a USB port on your ChromeBook.

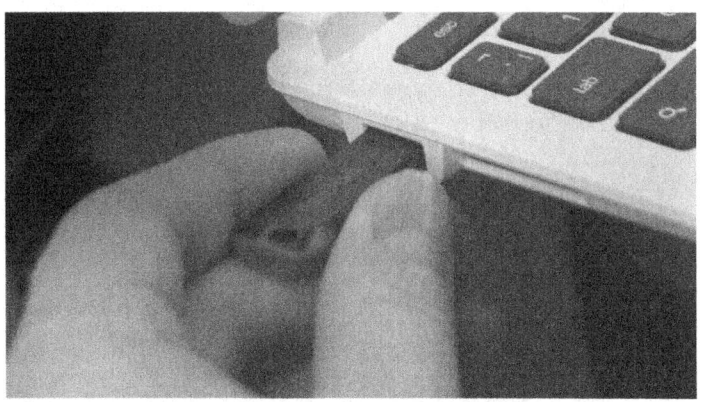

Now, on your ChromeBook, open 'files' from the app shelf. You'll also find it on your launcher.

Select your USB drive from the panel on the left hand side of the window.

Click and drag files to the USB drive.

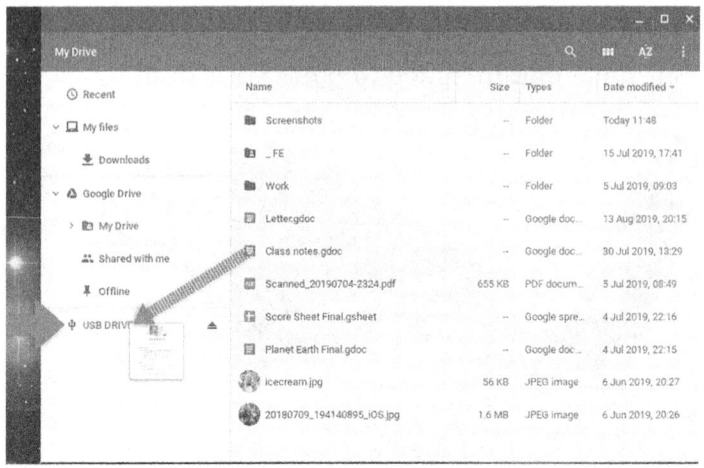

Quick Lock Your Screen

To quickly lock your screen, press the **search** key then tap the letter **'L'**.

You'll land on the lock screen page where you'll need to enter your password to unlock your screen.

Sign in as Guest

If you want to allow someone to use your Chromebook but don't want them to be able to access all your data, you can allow them to use your machine as a guest.

First you need to enable the feature. To do this, open your settings app, scroll down to the 'people' section. Click 'manage people'.

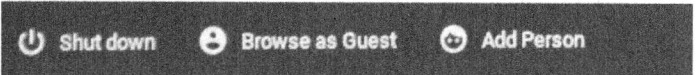

Click 'enable guest browsing'. Now on the login screen choose 'browse as guest'.

Taking Screenshots

To take a screenshot, hold down the control key, then tap the 'switch window' key.

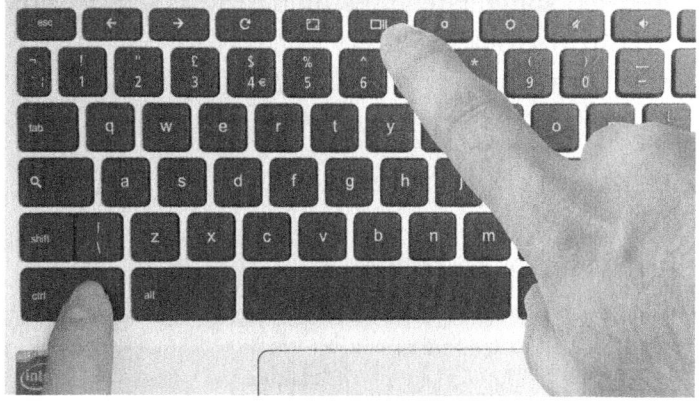

Screenshots will be saved in your downloads folder in the file app.

Change Desktop Wallpaper

Right click on your desktop. To do this, tap with two fingers on the touchpad.

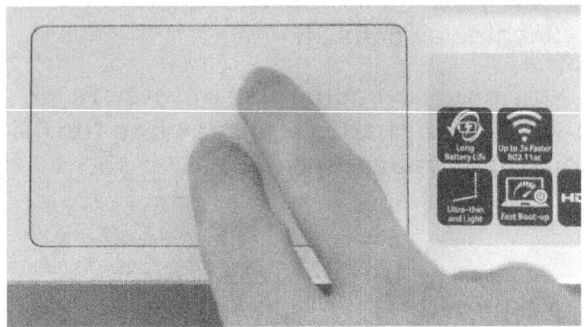

From the popup menu, select 'set wallpaper'.

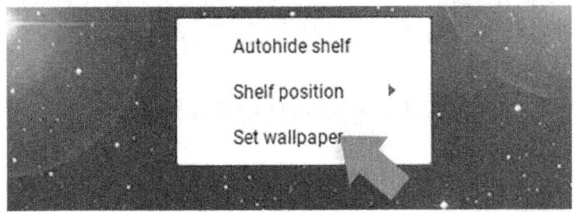

You'll see some categories along the left hand side of the window, select one.

Scroll down the thumbnail previews of all the wallpapers and click on one you like.

Photo as Desktop Wallpaper

If you want to add your own image, open Google Drive in your file explorer.

You'll find your file explorer on the shelf along the bottom of the screen. If it isn't there, you'll find the icon on your launcher on the far left hand side.

Browse through your photos - you'll find your photos in 'My Files' or 'Google Drive'.

Right click on the one you want to use (to right click, tap on the image with two fingers on the touch pad).

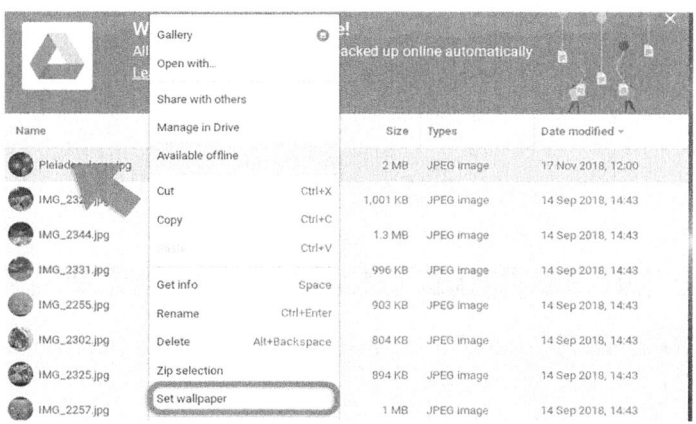

Creating Documents

You'll find Google Docs on your app launcher. Just click the icon to start the app.

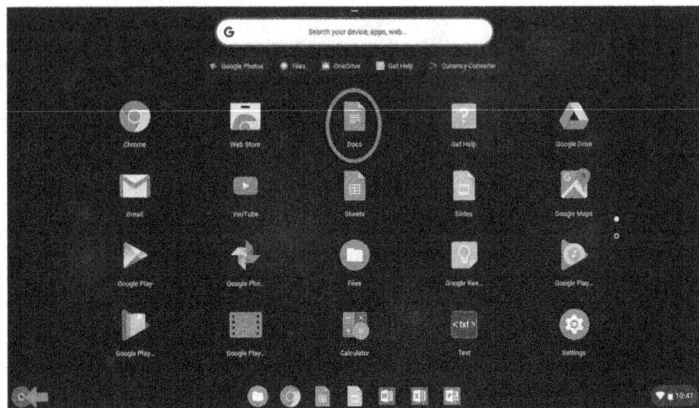

When Google Docs opens, you'll see the documents you have been working on recently. You can click any of these to re-open them. To create a new document, click the red + on the bottom right of the screen.

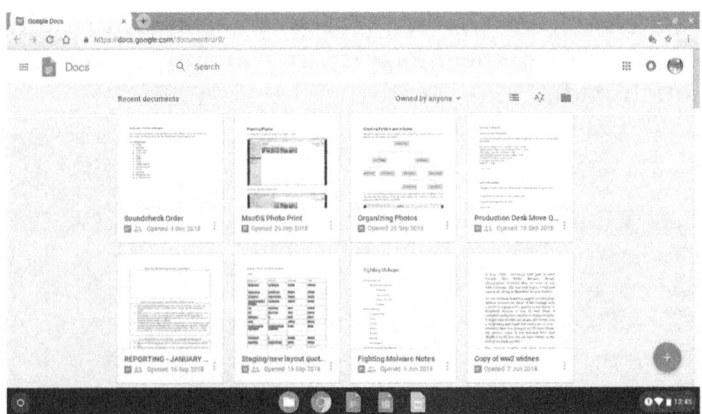

We'll start with a blank document. Click the red + on the bottom right.

Google Docs will open the main window where you can create your document.

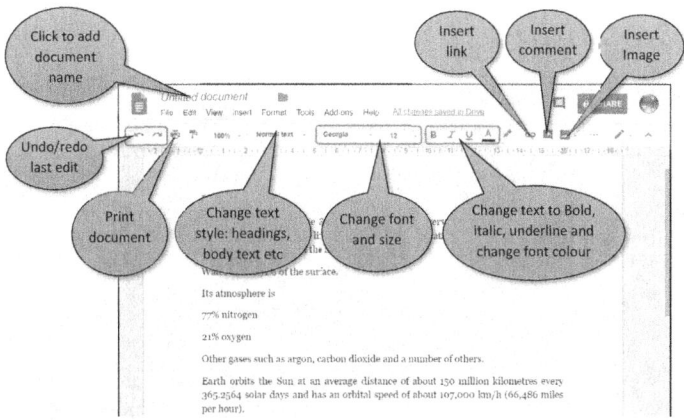

Along the top you'll see the document name. It's a good idea to rename this to something more meaningful that 'untitled document'. Click on the text and type in a name.

Underneath are the menus. This is where you'll find tools that are not represented as icons on the toolbar.

Under the menus you'll see the toolbar. This is where you'll find most of the tools you'll need to create and format your documents.

Creating Spreadsheets

You'll find Google Sheets on your app launcher. Just click the icon to start the app.

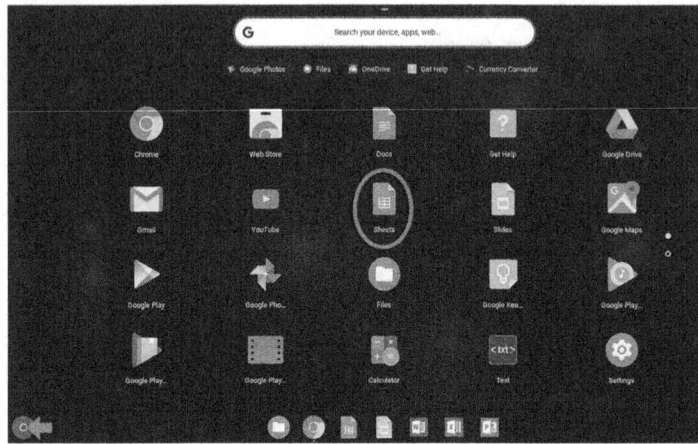

When Google Sheets opens, you'll see the spreadsheets you have been working on recently. You can click any of these to re-open them. To create a new spreadsheet, click the red + on the bottom right of the screen.

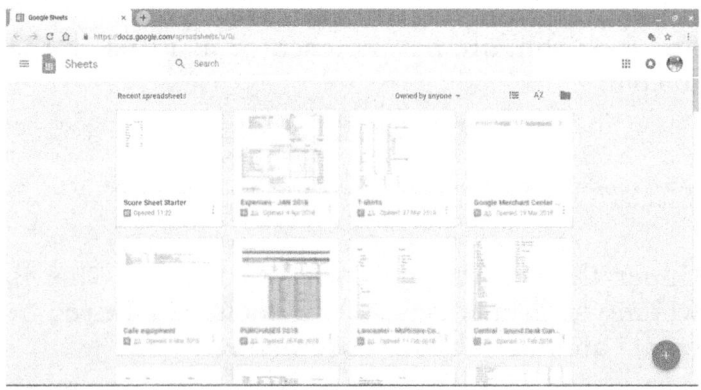

We'll start with a blank spreadsheet. Click the red + on the bottom right.

Google Sheets will open the main window where you can create your spreadsheet.

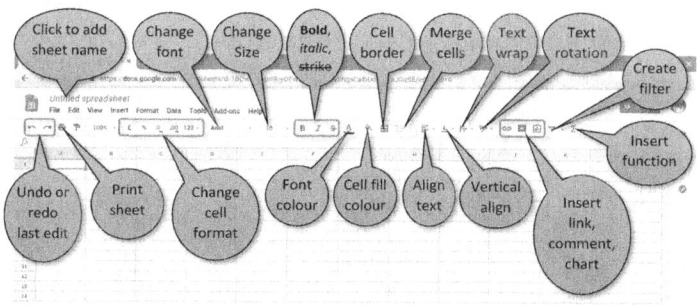

Along the top you'll see the spreadsheet name. It's a good idea to rename this to something more meaningful that 'untitled spreadsheet'. Click on the text and type in a name.

Underneath are the menus. This is where you'll find tools that are not represented as icons on the toolbar.

Under the menus you'll see the toolbar. This is where you'll find most of the tools you'll need to create and format your spreadsheets.

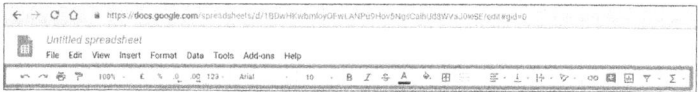

Then you have the formula bar *(fx)*. Here, you'll be able to see and add any functions or formulas in the selected cell.

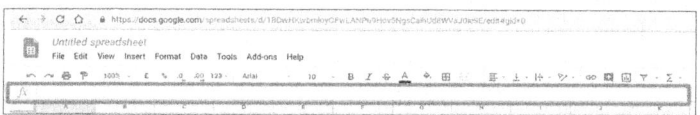

Creating Presentations

You'll find Google Slides on your app launcher. Just click the icon to start the app.

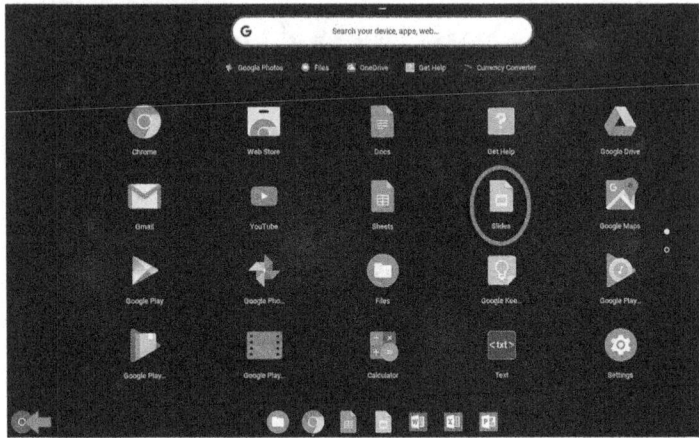

When Google Slides opens, you'll see the presentations you have been working on recently. You can click any of these to re-open them. To create a new presentation, click the red + on the bottom right of the screen.

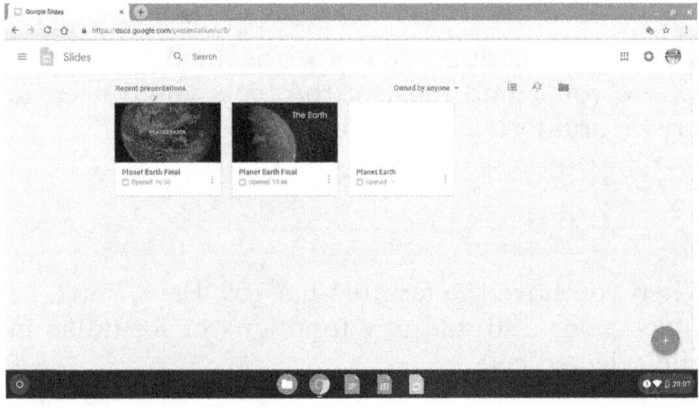

We'll start with a blank presentation. Click the red + on the bottom right.

Google Slides will open the main window where you can create your presentation.

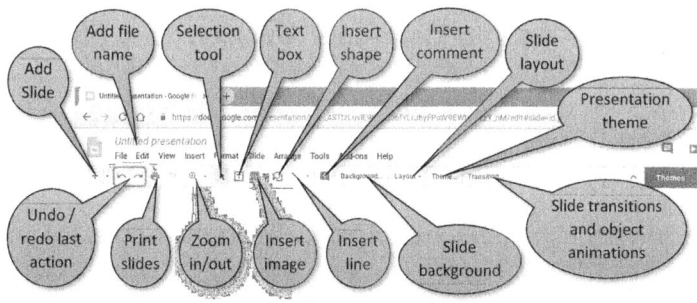

Along the top you'll see the presentation name. It's a good idea to rename this to something more meaningful that 'untitled presentation'. Click on the text and type in a name.

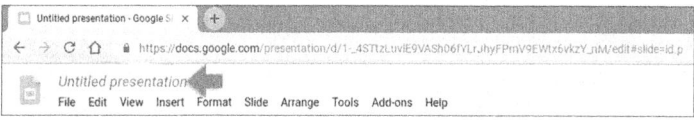

Underneath are the menus. This is where you'll find tools that are not represented as icons on the toolbar.

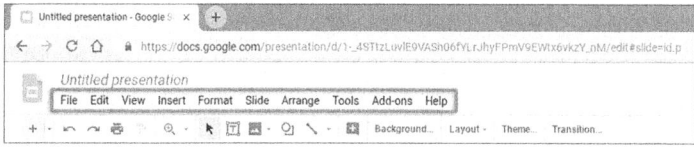

Under the menus you'll see the toolbar. This is where you'll find most of the tools you'll need to create and format your presentations.

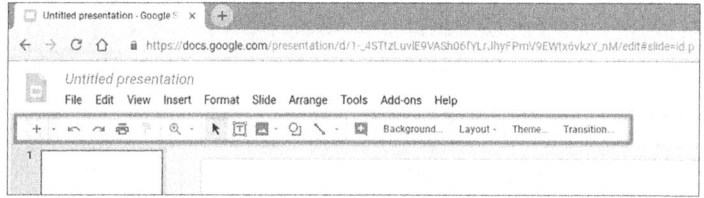

Using Google Drive

Google Drive is a cloud storage service developed by Google and encompasses Google Docs, Sheets, and Google, which are a part of Google's own office suite. Google Drive offers all users 15 gigabytes of free storage space but more is available through a subscription to Google One.

You can access Google Drive through the files app on your launcher.

You'll find a link on the left hand side. Click on it to open it up.

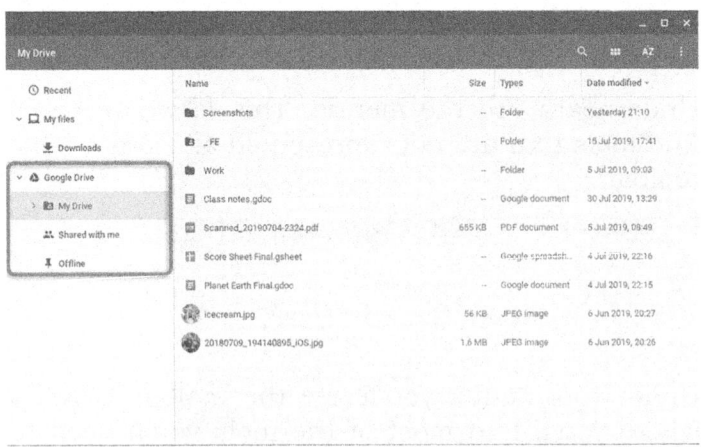

You'll see a list of any folders you've created on Google Drive under 'my drive', as well as any folders that have been shared with you by other users under 'shared with me'. In the right hand pane, you'll see a list of all the files in the folder selected in the left hand pane.

Google Drive on Any Device

You can run these apps on any computer or tablet that has access to the internet - it can be a mac, pc, or laptop. Using your web browser navigate to

drive.google.com

Sign in with your Google Account.

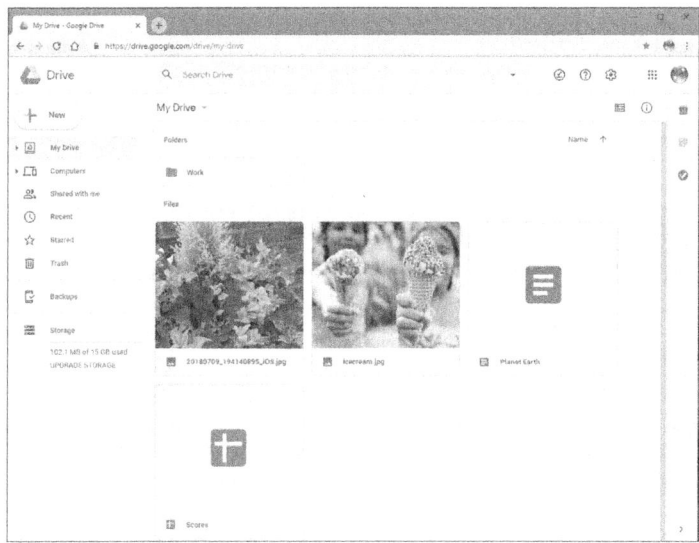

If you are on a phone or tablet, go to the app store on the device and download the Google Drive app.

You'll find the app on your home screen. Tap the icon to open it up.

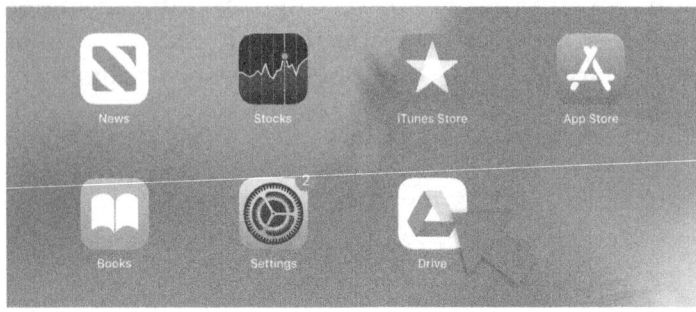

Once the app has loaded, you'll see your main screen.

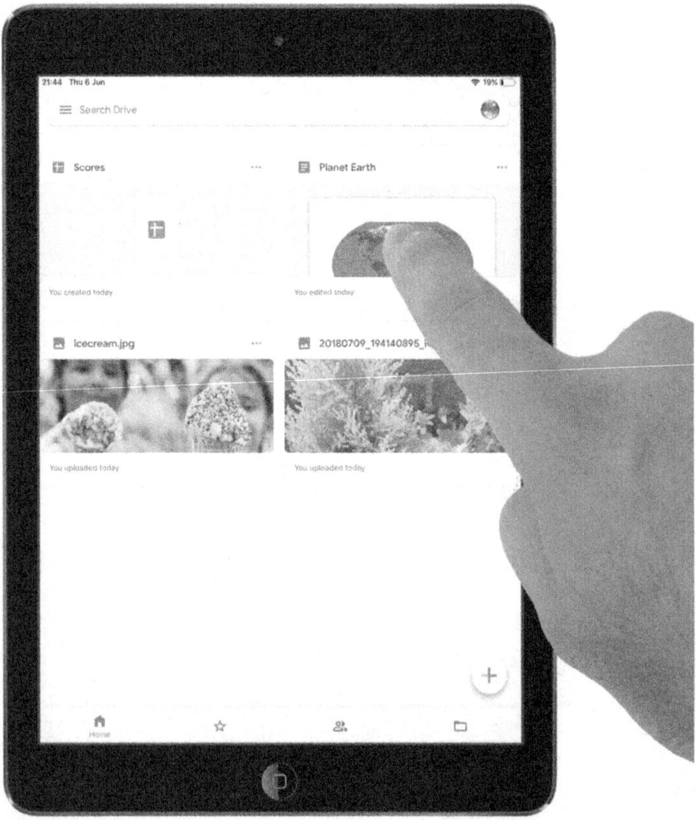

Working Offline

To get started, make sure offline sync is enabled in Google Drive:

While you're still connected to the internet, open your browser and navigate to:

drive.google.com

Click the settings icon on the top right.

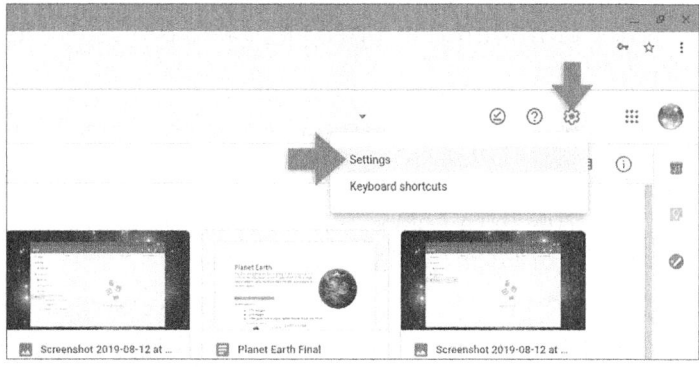

Click the box next to "Sync Google Docs, Sheets, Slides & Drawings files to this computer so that you can edit offline."

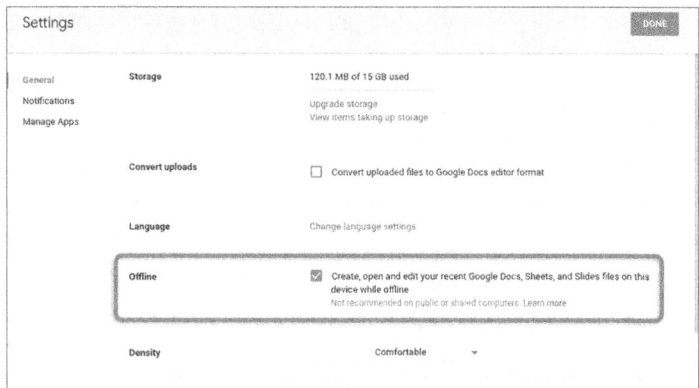

Allow Google Drive to sync, then you're all set.

Transferring Files

There are various ways to transfer your files over to your ChromeBook.

You can upload files to Google Drive directly from your old computer or device.

Note with Google Drive you get 15GB free. If you need any more, you'll need to pay a subscription fee.

On your old computer, open your web browser and navigate to

drive.google.com

Sign in with your Google Account, then from the Google Drive home page, click 'my drive' on the left hand side of your browser window.

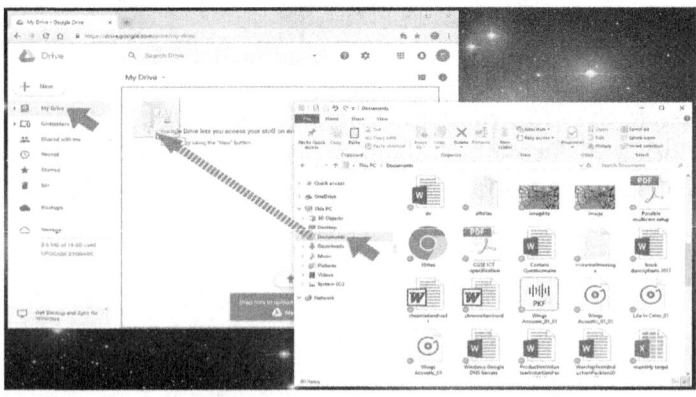

Now open file explorer and navigate to where your files are saved. This is usually under the 'this pc' section on the left hand side.

Click 'documents', then drag the folder over to the Google Drive home page, as shown above. It helps to position your windows side by side.

Bookmarking Websites

It is useful to bookmark, or favourite a site you visit frequently. To do this, navigate to the website you want to bookmark, then click the small star icon to the right of the address bar at the top of your window.

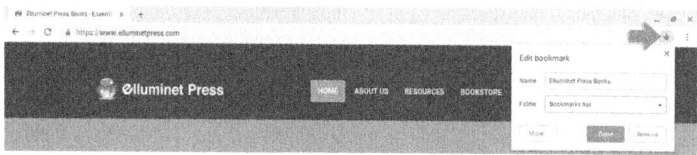

Enter a meaningful name in the 'name' field, if there isn't one. Add your bookmark to the bookmarks bar along the top of your screen. Click 'done' when you're finished.

Notice that your bookmarks bar isn't enabled by default. To enable the bar, click the three dots icon on the top right of the screen. From the drop down, go to 'bookmarks', then from the slideout menu, select 'show bookmarks bar'.

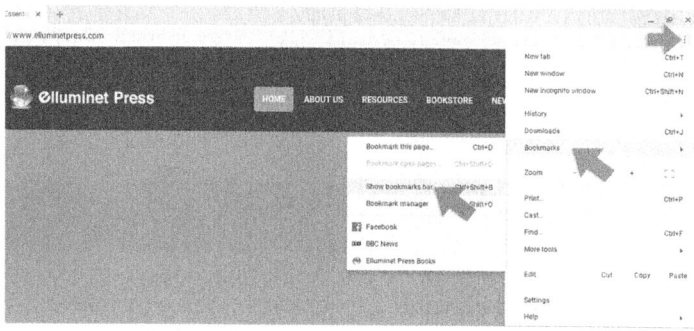

The bar will appear along the top of the screen underneath the address bar.

47

If you have a lot of bookmarked sites, the bookmarks bar can become very cluttered. To get around this, you can create folders on your bookmarks bar, to make it easier to find sites.

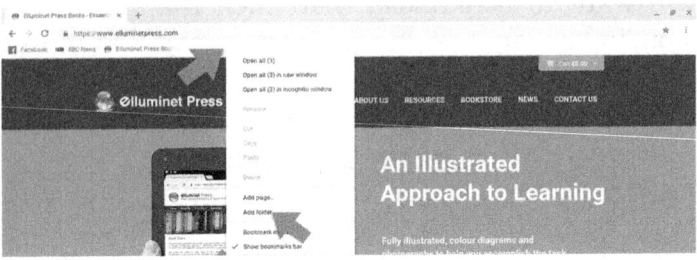

In the dialog box, type in the name of the folder and select 'bookmarks bar'.

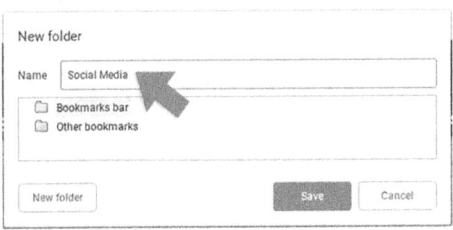

Click 'save' when you're done. You'll see your folder appear on the bookmarks bar.

Now you can drag the site bookmarks you want to put in this folder. For example, I'm going to add 'facebook' to the social media folder.

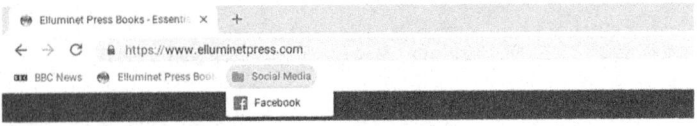

Printing Webpages

To print a webpage in Chrome, click the three dots icon on the top right of your screen, then from the drop down menu, select 'print'.

Check the printer 'destination', make sure your printer is selected. Click 'change' if you need to change this. Enter the pages you want to print, or leave it blank to print all of them. Enter the number of copies you want.

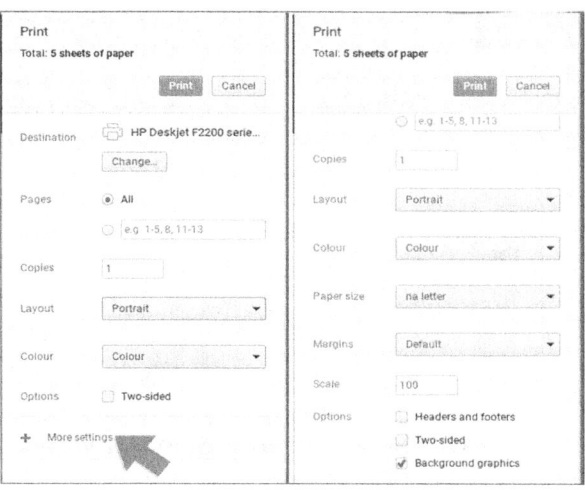

Click 'more settings'. Select the paper size if needed. Change the margins if the website doesn't fit on the page. Click 'background graphics' - this ensures all the graphics will print. Click 'print' when you're done.

Pin Websites to your Shelf

The Shelf is a good spot to keep your most-used apps, but you can also add links to your most used websites.

To do this navigate to the site you want in Chrome. Click on the three dots icon on the top right and select "More tools."

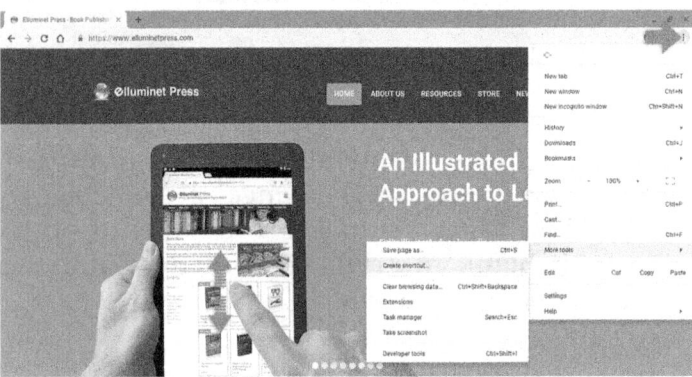

Click on "create shortcut" from the slideout menu. From the dialog box, click 'create'.

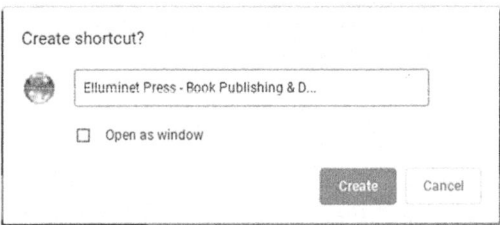

The website will be added to the end of your shelf.

Reading Email

GMail is where you'll be able to check your email. You'll find GMail on your app launcher.

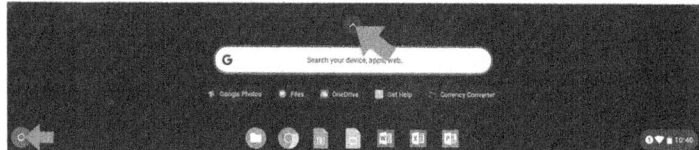

Open the app launcher fully and click the GMail icon.

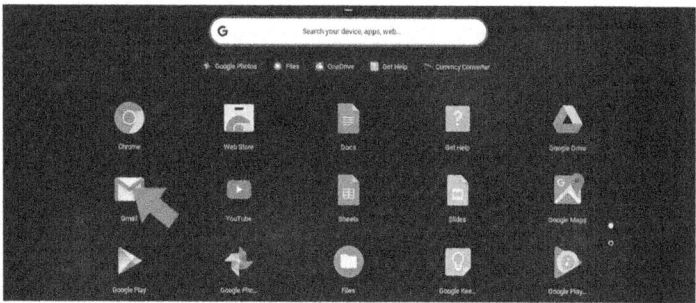

Once GMail opens, you'll be able to see the email messages sent to your Google Account email address. Let's take a look at the main screen.

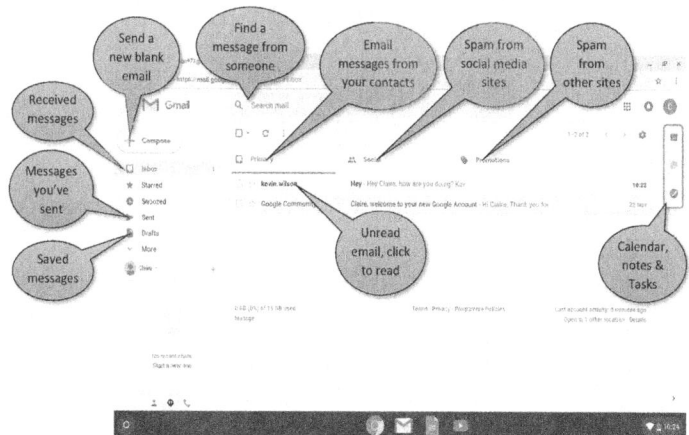

Emailing Attachments

To attach a file, click the paperclip icon along the bottom of your message. Use this option to attach files such as documents, videos, music, or multiple photos.

Select your file from the dialog box. Click the tick box on the top left of the images to select multiple files. Click 'open' when you're done.

These attachments will be added to the end of the email.

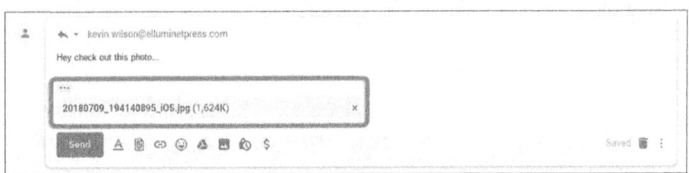

Insert an Image

Inserting images is a little different from adding an attachment. When you insert an image, you insert it into the body of the email message so it appears inline with the text.

In your email message, click the images icon from the bottom of your message.

Click 'upload' along the top of the window, if it isn't already selected. Select 'inline' from the two options on the bottom right of the window.

Click 'choose photos to upload'.

Select your file from the dialog box. Click the tick box on the top left of the images to select multiple files. Click 'open' when you're done.

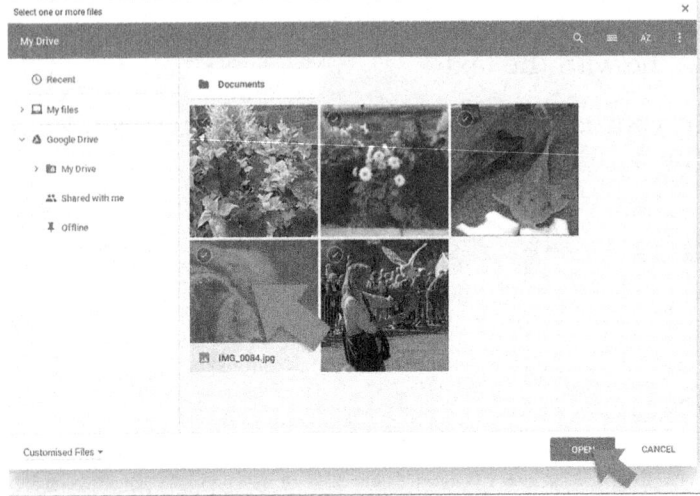

Notice the photo has been inserted within the text body of your email, rather than just attached to the end as an attachment.

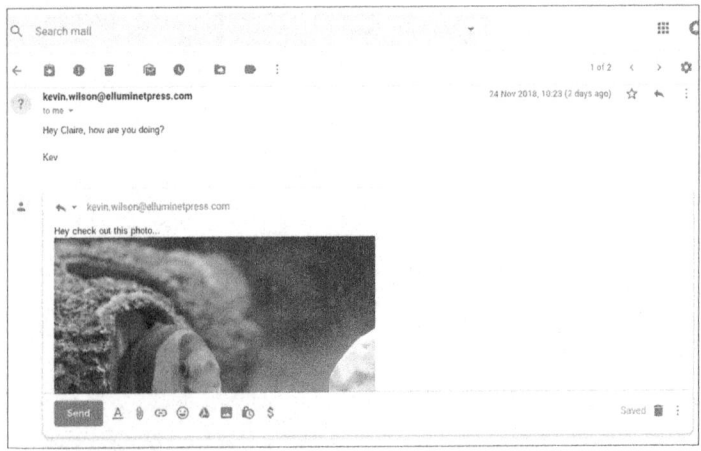

Click the 'send' icon on the top right when you're done.

Add Other Email Accounts

In the top right, click the 'settings' icon, then select 'settings' from the menu.

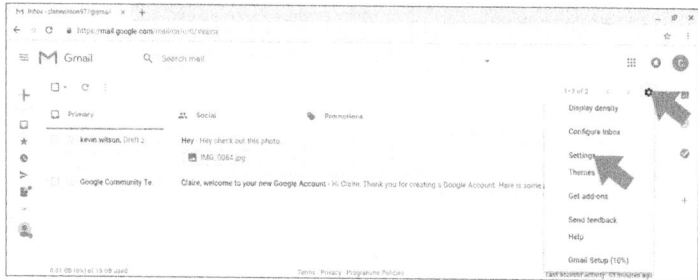

Click 'accounts and import', then select 'add an email account'.

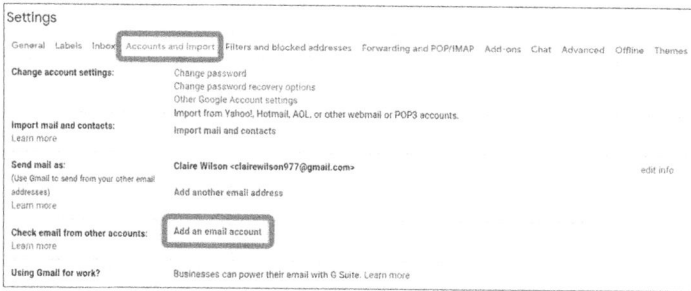

In the dialog box that appears, enter the email address of the account you want to add.

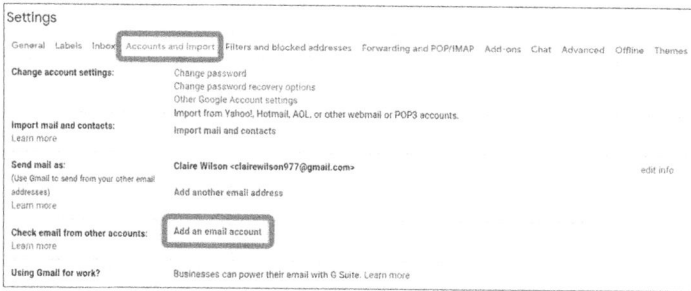

Click 'next'.

Select 'link accounts with Gmailify' if available, then click 'next'.

Sign in with the password for the account you're adding.

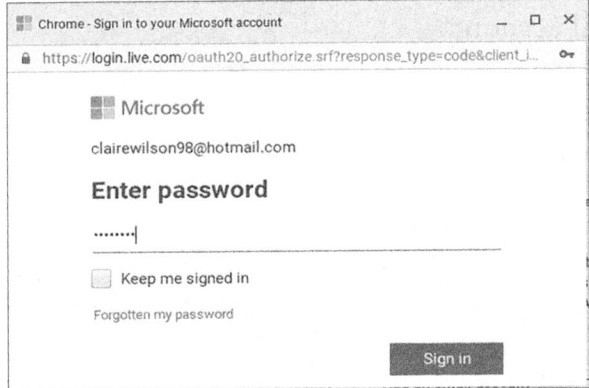

Click 'yes' to grant access to the email account you're adding.

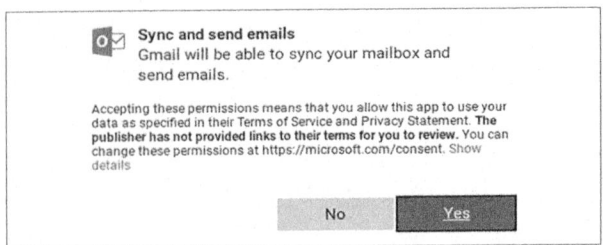

Click 'close' on the last dialog box, and you're done.

Add Contact from Message

You can add a new contact from the Hangouts App or the GMail App

Open the email.

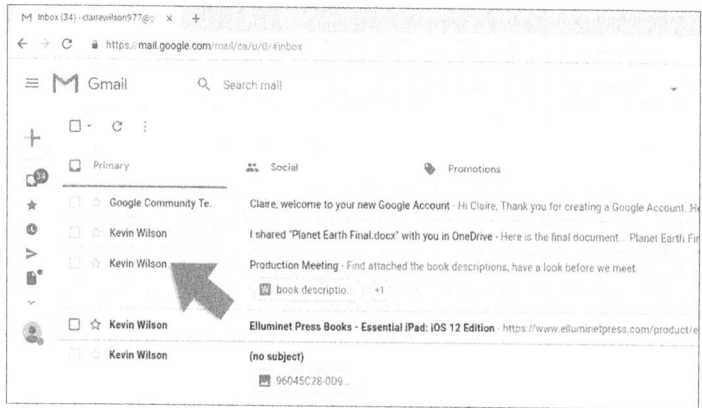

Click on the three dots icon on the top right of your email message, then select 'add ... to contacts list'.

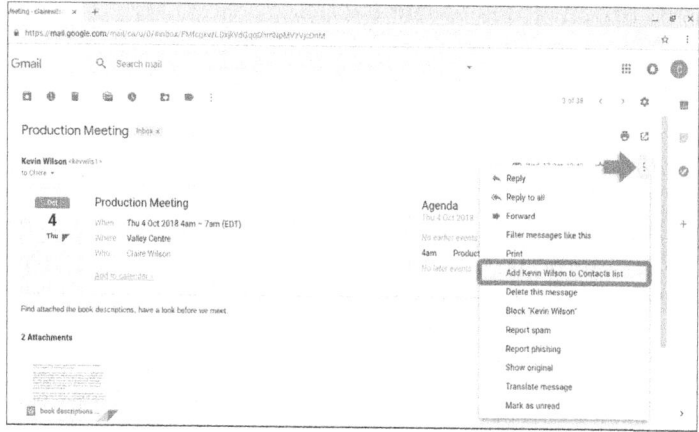

The email address and the person's name will be added to your contacts. Click on the contact's name in your contacts app to edit any details.

Add Event to Calendar

To add a new event, reminder or appointment, in month view, click on the day the appointment falls on.

In the popup box, start typing in the name of the event or appointment in the field at the top. Eg "production meeting", "coffee with claire", and so on. Select 'event', then click 'more options'.

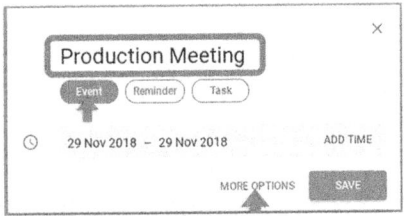

Remove the tick from 'all day' and enter the start and finish times of the event.

If this event repeats, for example, a weekly meeting, click where it says 'doesn't repeat' and from the drop down, select how often the event repeats. This event occurs every week, so I'm going to select 'weekly'.

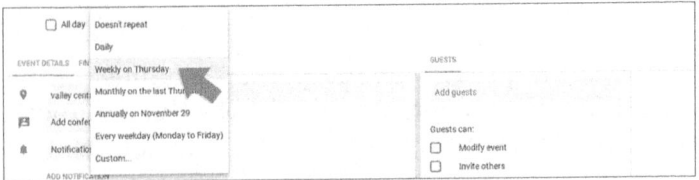

Now select where the event/appointment will be held. Type in the location.

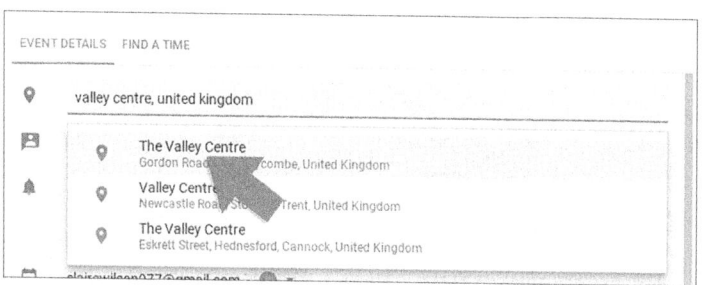

Google will search for places you've been, go to frequently, or places nearby. Click on one of these. So if we were meeting at the Valley Centre, I'd click on 'valley centre' in the list.

You'll see a summary of the appointment. Here you can amend any details, set a reminder - where it says 'notification', change the times - select how far in advance you want to be reminded. In this example, I've set it to remind me a day before. You can also set it to 30 mins before, an hour before, and so on.

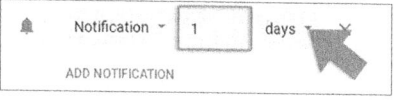

Now we need to say who we are meeting. Click where it says 'add guests' on the right hand side.

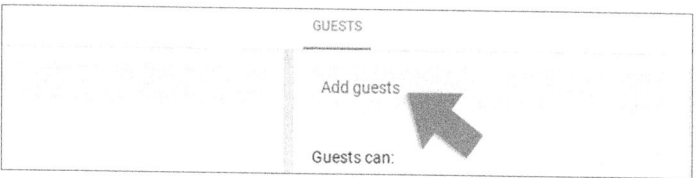

Start typing in the names of the people you want to send an invite to. You'll see a list of your contacts - select their name.

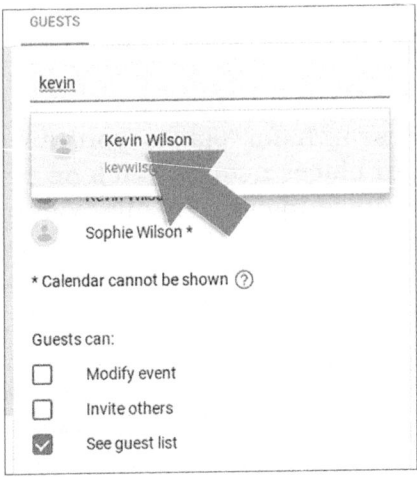

Underneath where it says 'guests can', remove the ticks from the permissions to prevent your guests from making changes to the event invitation. You can allow them to 'see the guest list' so they can see who is attending.

At the bottom left, where it says 'add description'. Add a message, and any attachments, or documents needed for the event. These could be minutes, meeting notes, programmes, and so on. To add an attachment, click the paper-clip icon, then select a file to attach.

Click the blue 'save' button on the top right when you're done.

Call Someone on Hangouts

To place a new video call, click the video icon in the middle of the screen.

Enter the name or GMail address of the person you're calling. Click the correct name from the drop down list.

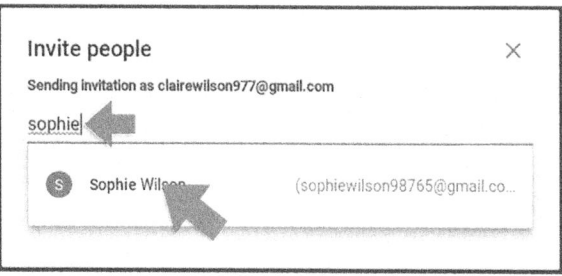

Click 'invite'.

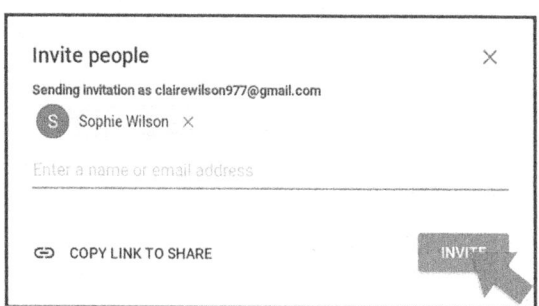

The other person will get a prompt on their hangouts window.

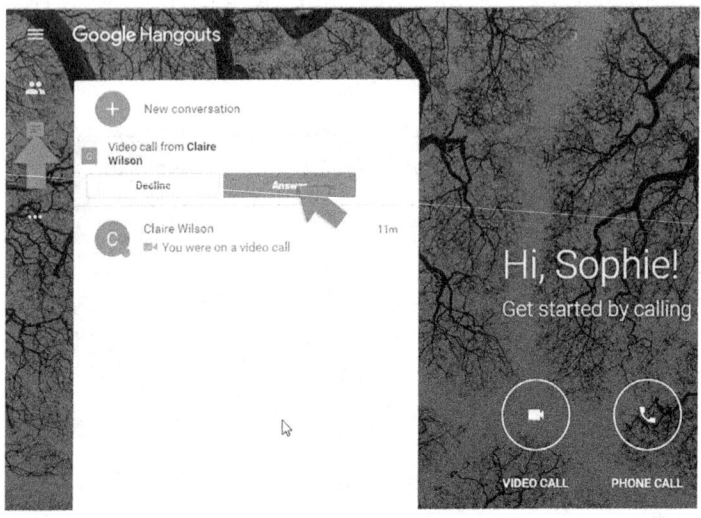

Now you can have a video conversation with that person.

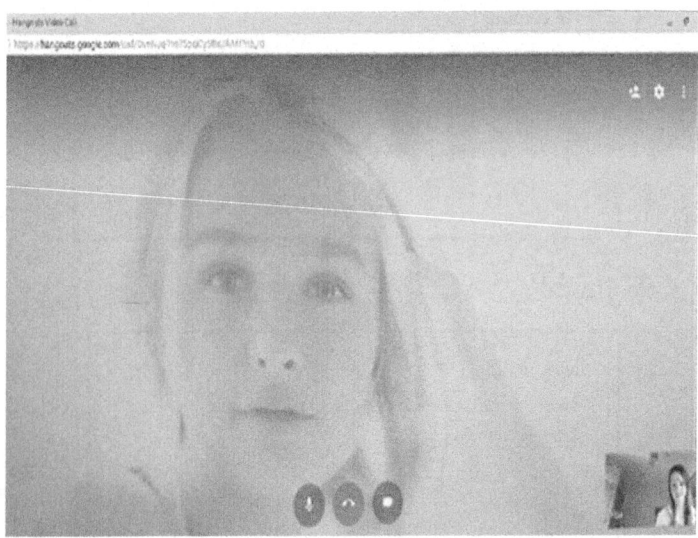

Integrate DropBox

If you have a DropBox account, you can integrate the service into the Files app on your Chromebook.

To do this, open the Files app, click the three-dot icon in its top-right corner, then select 'Add new service'.

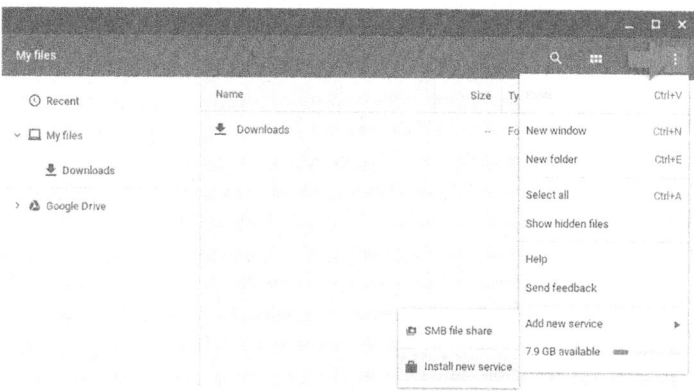

Select 'install' next to the DropBox service.

Click 'mount your DropBox', then sign in with your DropBox username and password

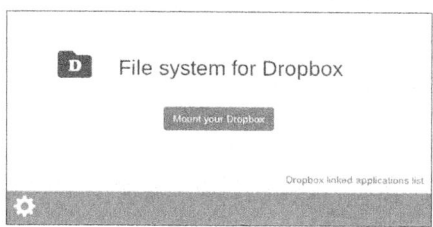

You'll find your DropBox listed down the left hand side of your Files app.

Integrate OneDrive

If you have a OneDrive account, you can integrate the service into the Files app on your Chromebook. To do this, open the Files app, click the three-dot icon in its top-right corner, then select 'Add new service'.

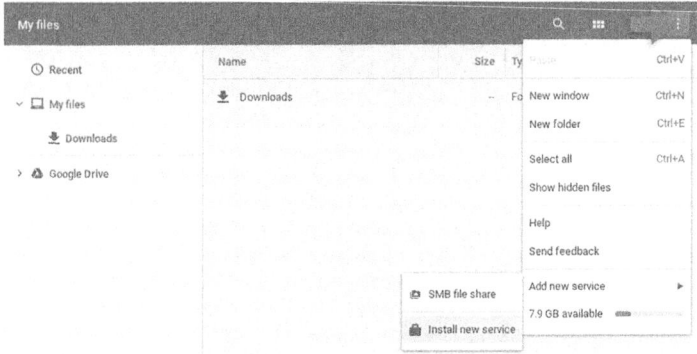

Select 'install' next to the OneDrive service.

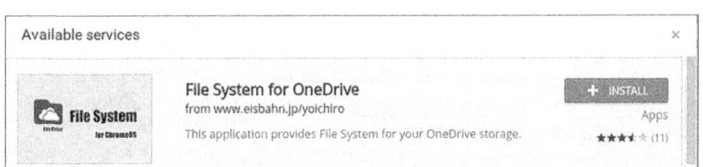

Click 'mount', then sign in with your Microsoft Account username and password

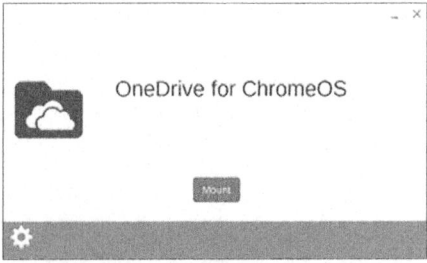

You'll find your OneDrive listed down the left hand side of your Files app.

Remote Desktop

You can access another computer remotely such as your Windows PC, or Mac from your Chromebook. First you need to set it up.

On the machine you want to remotely access (eg your Windows PC), open Google Chrome and navigate to the following website:

`remotedesktop.google.com`

Scroll down the page, click 'get started'. Sign in with your Google Account.

Click the blue download icon to install the remote desktop chrome extension.

Click 'add to chrome', and accept any confirmation prompts.

Click 'accept and install'.

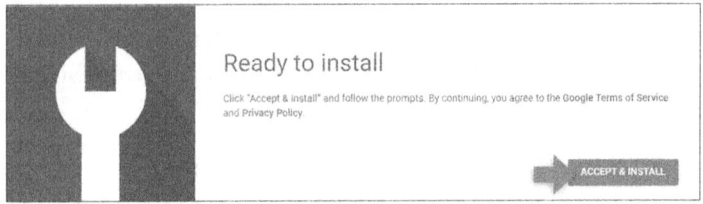

Type in a name for your computer, then click 'next'.

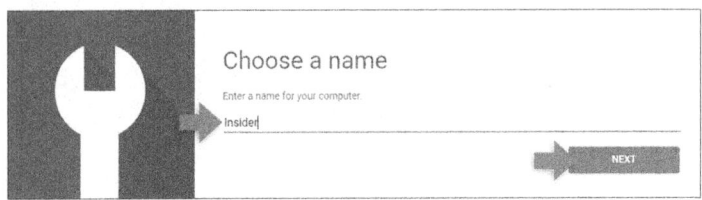

Enter a PIN code to secure your PC. Click 'start'.

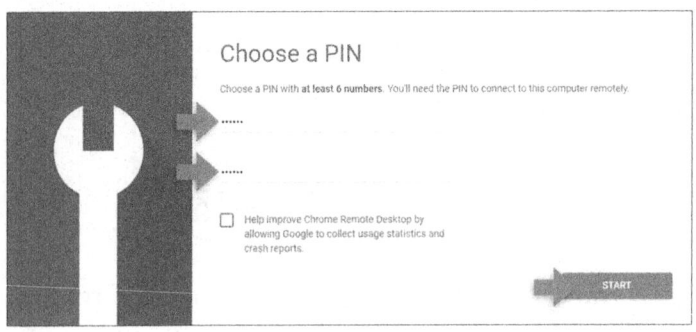

Note your PC will have to stay on for this to work.

Now on your Chromebook, open Chrome browser and navigate to the following website and sign in:

```
remotedesktop.google.com
```

At the top of the page, you'll see your computers. Click on the one you want to use.

Enter the PIN code you created earlier.

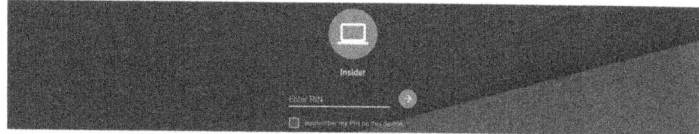

Now you can use your PC on your Chromebook.

Reset with Powerwash

If you want to clear your data off your Chromebook, you can use the power wash feature.

Note that this process removes all your data that is stored on your Chromebook. This will not affect anything stored on Google Drive.

To use Powerwash, open settings. Scroll down to the bottom of the 'advanced' settings until you see 'powerwash'. Click 'powerwash'.

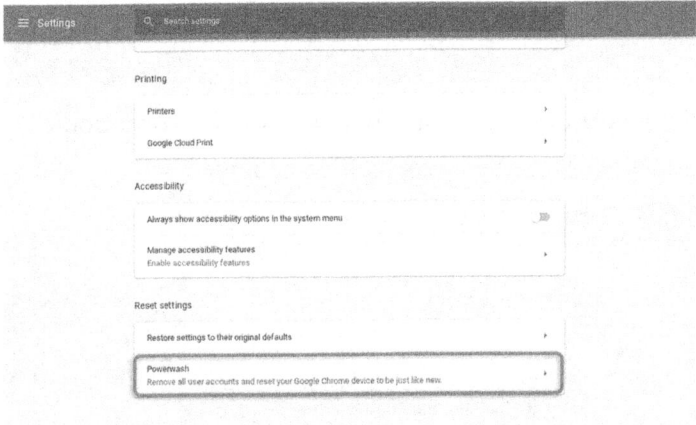

Then click 'restart'.

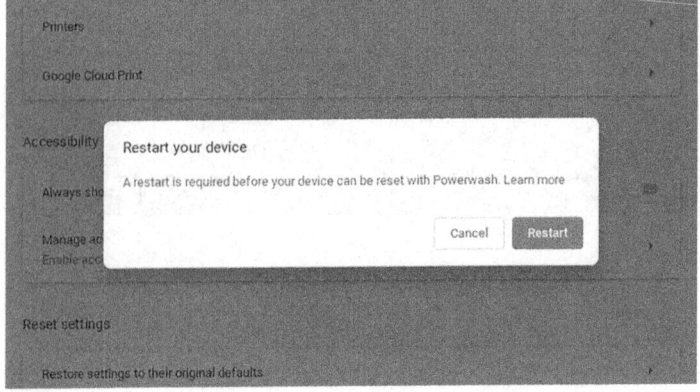

Keep Chromebook up to Date

Google release updates to their Chromebooks all the time. To make sure you're using the latest release, open your settings then click the hamburger icon on the top left.

From the side panel that opens up, scroll down the list and select 'about chrome OS'.

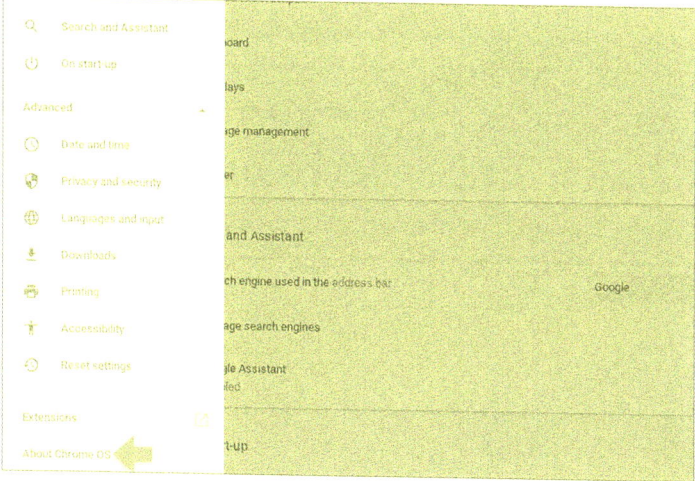

Click 'check for updates'.

Download Chrome Apps

This is where you can download countless apps for your ChromeBook. Many of these apps are free, but there are one or two that you will have to pay for. To launch the website, open your app launcher

Click the arrow at the top to open the launcher fully. Click 'web store'.

Once the web store opens, you'll see the home screen. Here, you can browse for apps and search for specific apps.

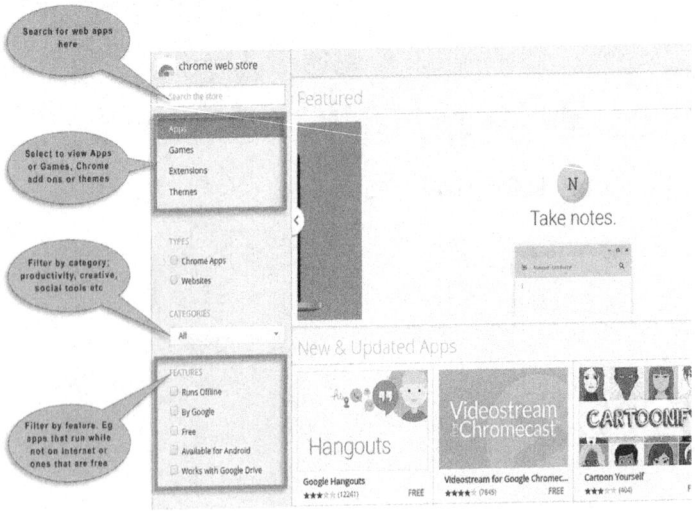

On the top left hand side of the store, you'll see a search field.

Click in the search field and type what you're looking for. You can use the app's name if you know it, or you can type something more generic such as 'word processing', or 'social media'. You'll also see a list of suggestions appear as you type - you can click any of these. Press the enter key on your keyboard to execute the search.

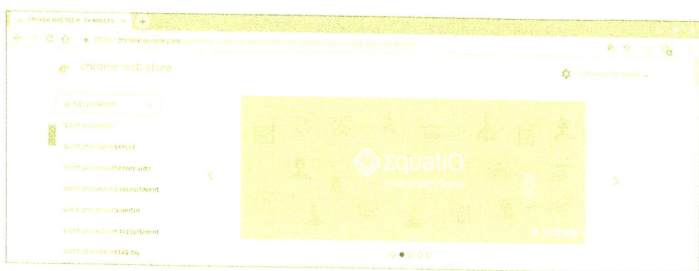

The Web Store will return a list of apps matching your search. You'll see the most popular apps in the list. To see all the apps, click 'more extensions' or 'more apps' on the top right of the screen.

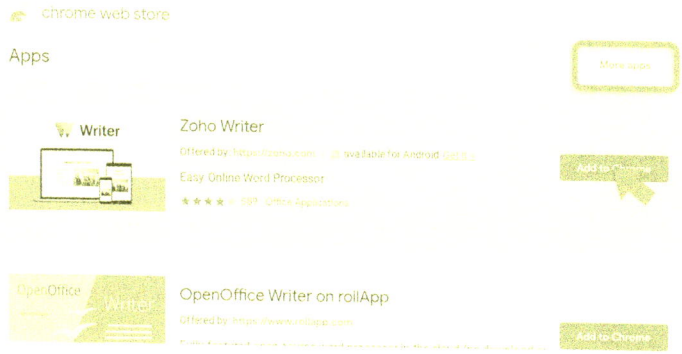

71

Downloading new apps is fairly straightforward. Once you have searched for and found the app you want, click on the thumbnail icon.

Once the info screen appears, you'll see a write up of the app with some screen shots and features. On the top right of your screen, you'll see a couple of icons. To install the app tap 'add to chrome'

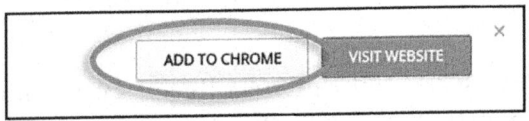

Then click 'add app' to install

You will see the app icon added to your App Launcher.

Listen to Music

Using the play music app you can purchase individual tracks and albums from the play store, or you can stream any music you like if you subscribe to 'play music'.

Click the app launcher icon on the bottom left, then click the arrow in the top middle to open it up fully.

Click the 'play music' icon.

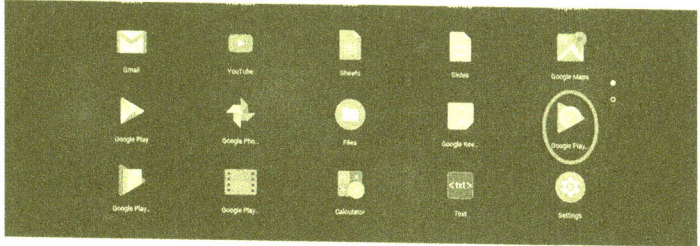

Google play music will open in Google Chrome.

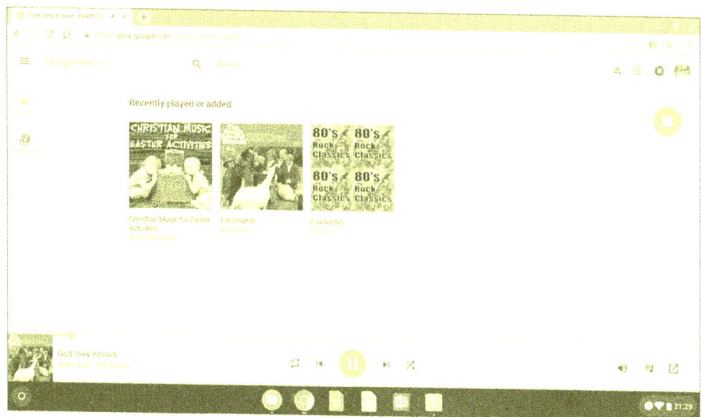

To download tracks and albums, you'll need to go to the Google Play Store.

Open the Google Play Store from your app launcher, and select 'music' from the selections listed down the left hand side

From here, you can browse through the latest releases and best selling tracks and albums. You can also use the search field at the top of the screen to find the songs, artists, or albums you want. Press enter on your keyboard to execute the search.

Browse through the search results and click the album or track you want.

At the top of the screen, you'll see a write up of the album. Click the price tag to purchase and download the entire album.

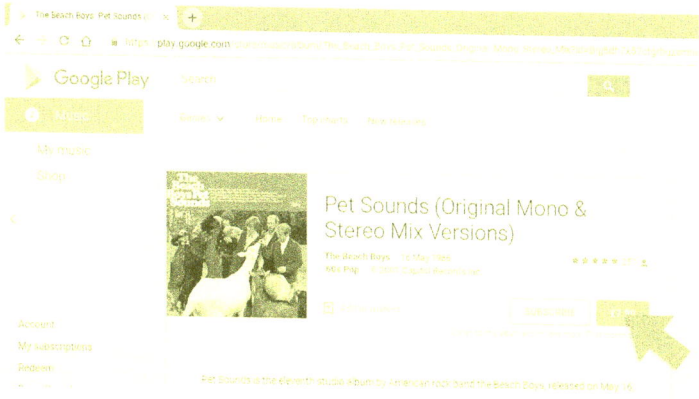

If you just want an individual track, scroll down the page and you'll come across a track list. This is a list of all the available tracks on the album.

Hover your mouse pointer over the track number on the left hand side, and click the play icon that appears to hear a sample of the track.

Click the price tag on the right to purchase and download the track.

You'll find the track/album in the Google Play Music App.

Streaming Music

You can subscribe to Google Play Music family plan for a monthly fee and have access to millions of tracks and albums available. You can sign up for an individual account, which allows one person to access the Google Music Library, or you can select the family plan and allow up to 6 people to access the Google Music Library at a time from their own devices.

To sign up, select the Google Play Music app from your launcher.

Click the hamburger icon on the top left hand side of your screen to reveal the menus.

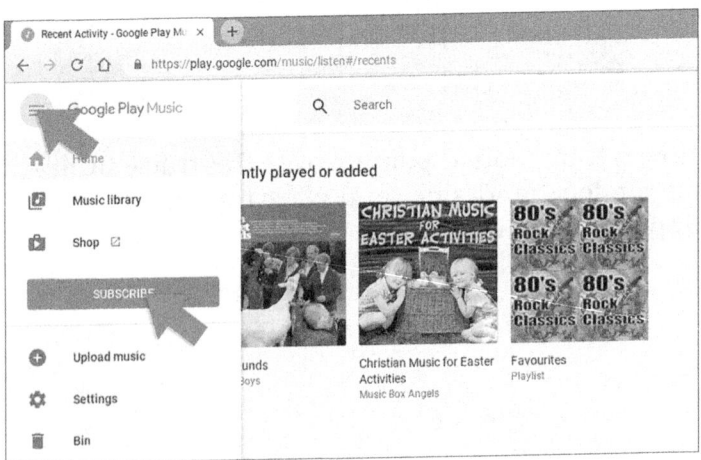

Select 'subscribe'.

Follow the instructions on the screen to sign up to the streaming service.

Send Music to Other Device

If you have a ChromeCast device, you can 'cast' music to your TV or other ChromeCast enabled speakers.

When playing a track, you'll see the ChromeCast icon on the play bar.

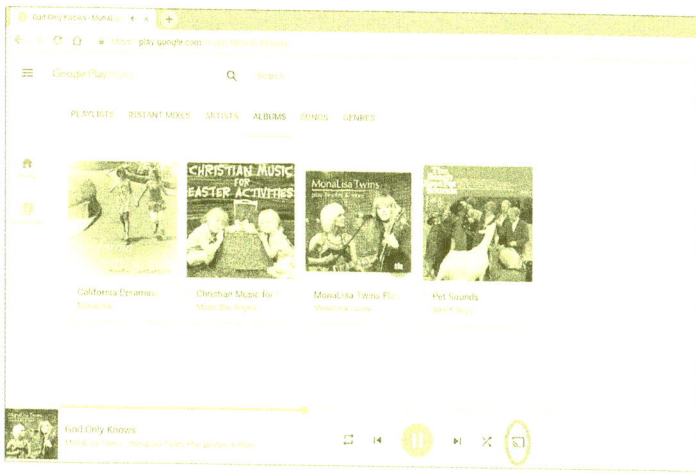

Select the device you want to cast to from the list.

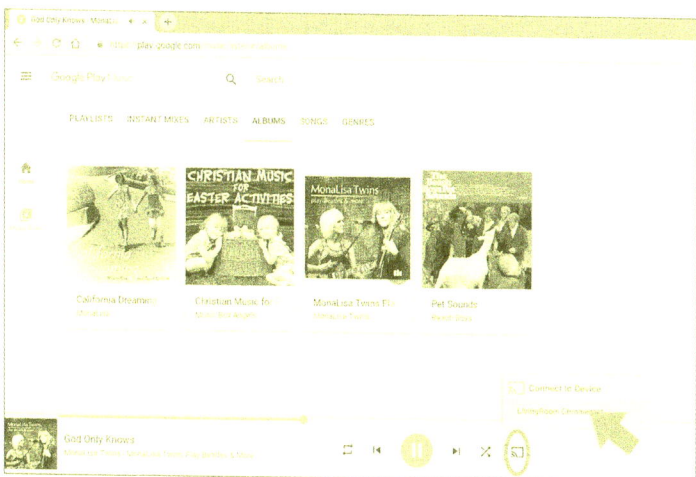

Find your Favourite Movie

Using the play movies app you can purchase or rent movies from the play store.

Click the app launcher icon on the bottom left, then click the arrow in the top middle to open it up fully.

Click the Google play music & TV icon.

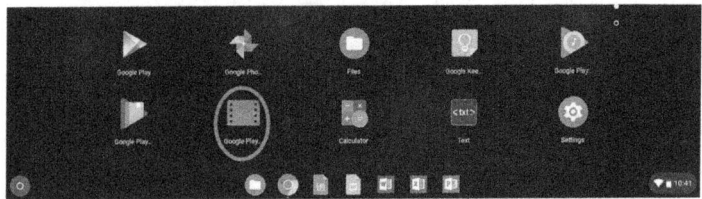

Google play movies & TV app will open.

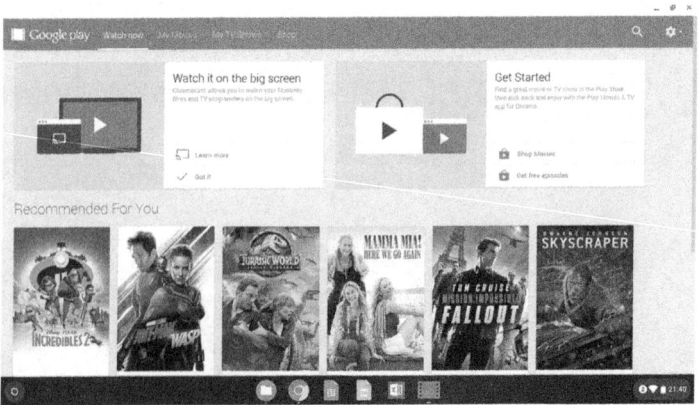

Here you'll see any movies or tv programmes you have downloaded, as well as the latest movies and tv shows for you to buy.

From the movies & TV section of the Google Play store, you can search for your favourite movies, actors, and genres using the search field at the top of the screen.

In the search results you'll see movies matching the search you entered. Click on one of the thumbnail covers to view details.

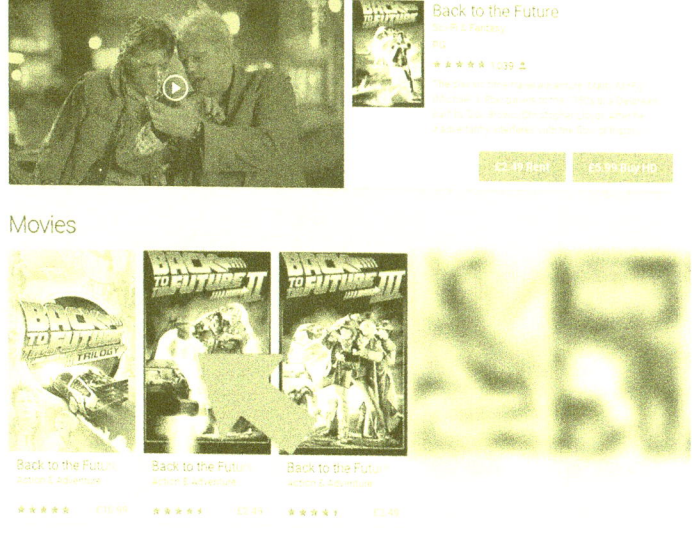

Here, you'll be able to read a write up of the movie, read reviews, see casts lists, and watch trailers.

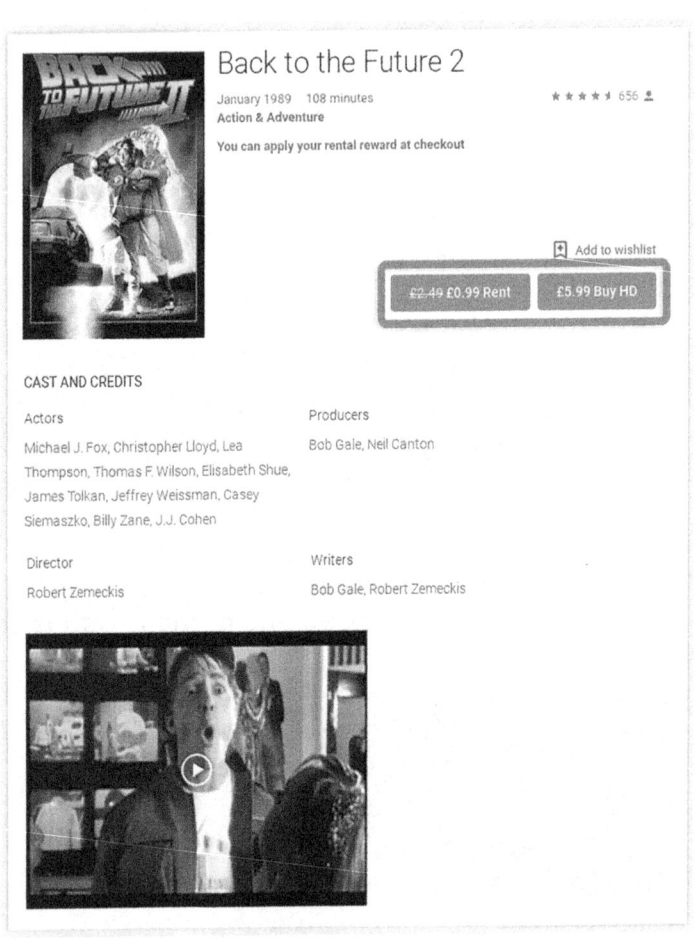

To buy the movie, click the 'buy' price tag. Some movies are available for rent. This allows you to download for 48 hours.

Watching Movies

Open the Play Movies & TV app from your app launcher.

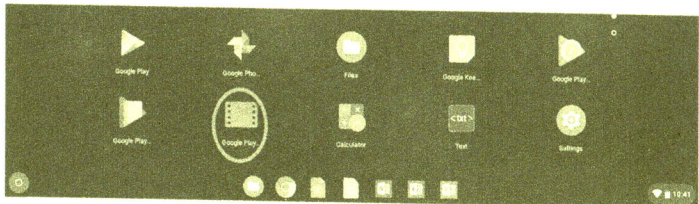

Click 'my movies' on the red panel at the top of the screen.

Click the thumbnail cover of the movie you want to watch.

On the movie details page, click play to start your movie.

Click on the full screen icon, sit back and enjoy your movie.

You can also cast your film to a TV or Projector, or you can connect to it using an HDMI cable, and watch your movie on a big screen.

Use ChromeCast

To use ChromeCast, first you'll need to buy a ChromeCast device, and plug it into an HDMI port on your TV or projector.

With ChromeCast you can stream from Netflix and YouTube, as well as any movie, TV show, or app from the Google Play Store. You can also use it to stream anything from Chrome browser on your ChromeBook.

Both your ChromeCast device and your ChromeBook will need to be on the same wifi network for it to work.

To cast a video you've downloaded from the Google Play store, open the Google Play Movies & TV app.

Select 'my movies' from the red bar along the top of the screen, then click on the movie you want to watch.

Play the movie, then tap the 'cast' icon on the top right hand side of the screen, then select your Chromecast device from the device list.

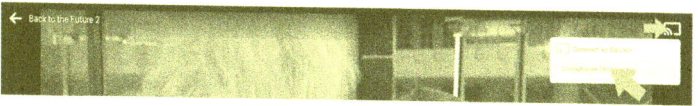

Watch TV Programs

From the movies & TV section of the Google Play store, you can search for your TV shows, actors, and genres using the search field at the top of the screen.

From the Google Play store, select 'movies & TV' from the list on the left hand side, then select 'tv'.

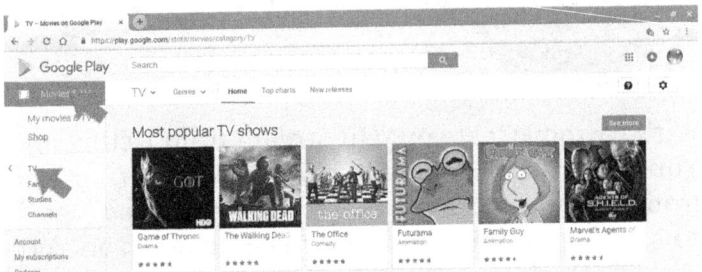

Type your search into the field at the top of the screen.

From the search results select 'see episodes'.

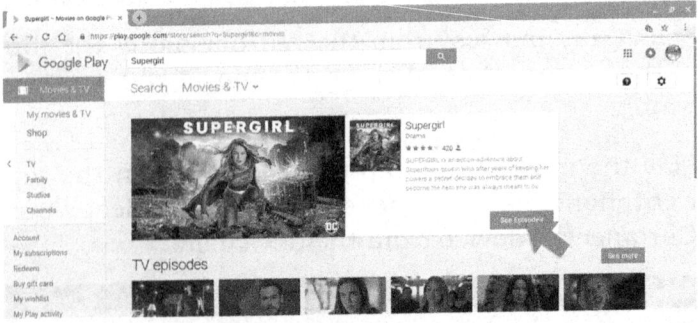

Select an episode to download and watch.

Watch Youtube

You'll find the youtube app on your app launcher which links directly to the website.

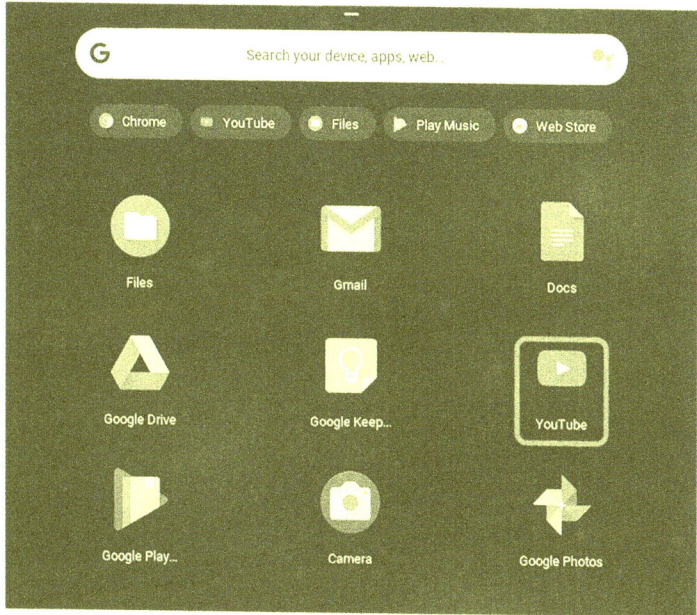

You can search as normal for anything you want to watch.

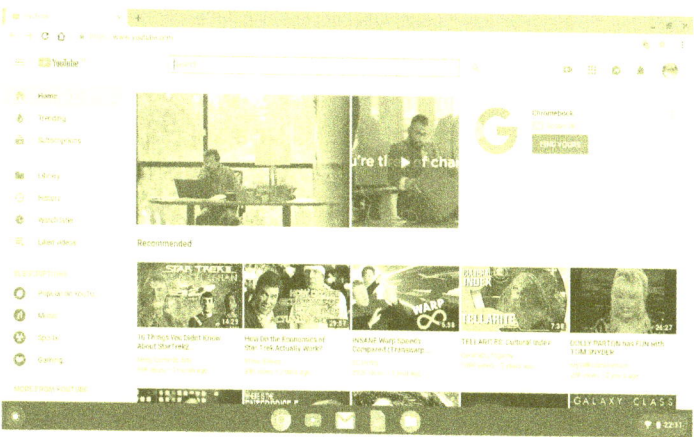

Read a Book

With the books app you can buy and read ebooks in a wide variety of different genres from the play store.

Click the app launcher icon on the bottom left, then click the arrow in the top middle to open it up fully.

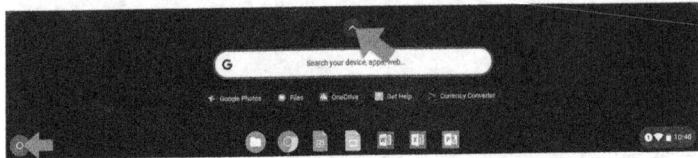

Click the Google play books icon.

Google play books will open in Google Chrome.

Here you'll see any books you have downloaded. Click the thumbnail book cover to open.

Download More Books

To download new eBooks, you'll need to go to the Google Play Store. Open the Google Play Store from your app launcher, and select 'books' from the selections listed down the left hand side.

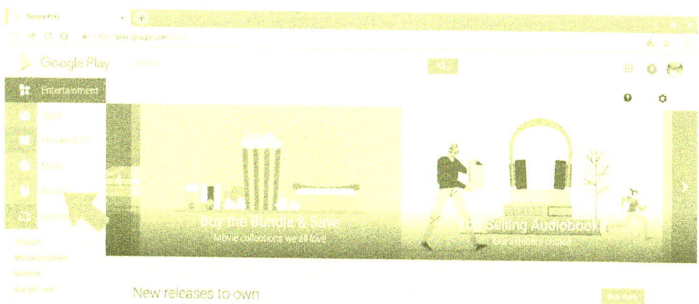

From here, you can browse through the latest releases and best selling books in various genres. You can also use the search field at the top of the screen to find book titles or authors you want. Press enter on your keyboard to execute the search.

Browse through the search results, click 'see more' on the top right to see all the results. Click on a book cover thumbnail to view details of the book.

Click 'buy ebook' to confirm.

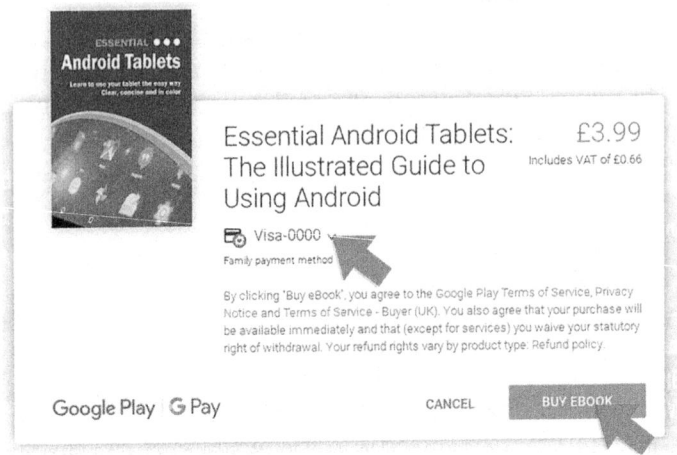

You'll find the ebooks you download in the Google Play Books app on your app launcher.

Click on one to open it up.

Opening Photos

With the photos app you can manage, store and enhance the photographs you take with your camera. You can also share photos on social media, or send them to friends and family.

Click the app launcher icon on the bottom left, then click the arrow in the top middle to open it up fully.

Click the Google photos icon.

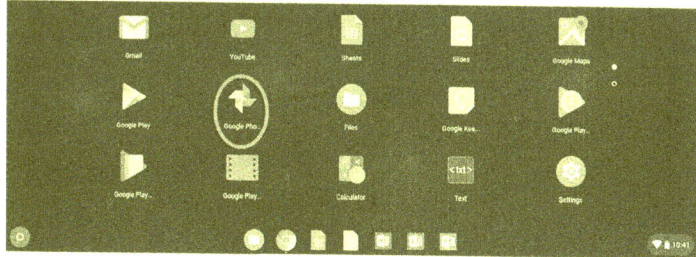

Google Photos will open in Google Chrome.

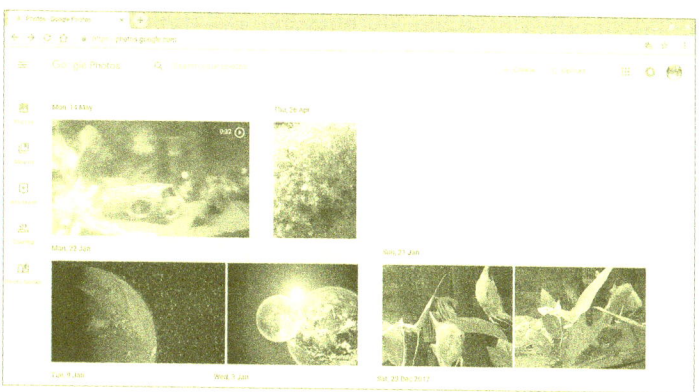

Add Filters to Photos

To adjust a photo, select it from the photos section or album. The photo will open up. Click the adjustments icon on the top right.

You'll see a panel on the right hand side of the screen. The panel is divided into three sections: filters, lighting adjustments, and crop/rotate.

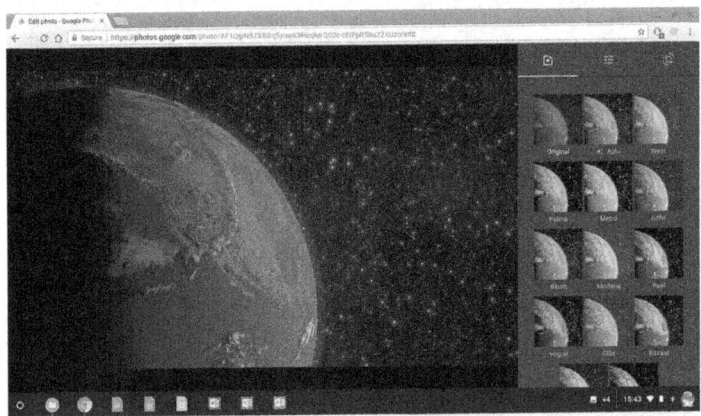

Enhancing Photos

To make adjustments to the lighting, contrast, or colour, click the centre icon on the top middle of the panel on the right hand side of the screen.

To change the general lighting and colour settings, move the 'light' and 'colour' sliders. To make the image pop off the page, use the 'pop' slider - try it see what happens.

To make more detailed changes to the lighting and contrast, click the small arrow next to the 'light' slider to open up the options.

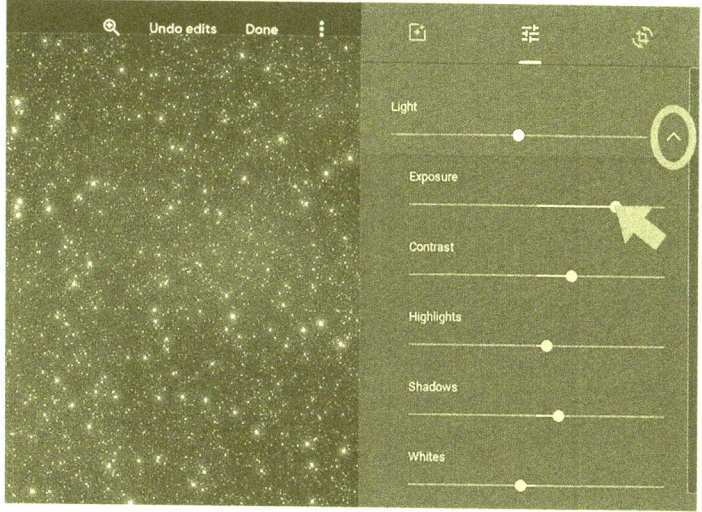

Use the individual sliders to adjust the different parts of the image. So...

- Exposure, lightens and darkens the whole image.
- Contrast is the difference between the dark and light parts of the image. Increasing the contrast can make parts of your image stand out.
- Highlights and whites, lighten and darken just the bright parts of the image. Eg you could darken the sky in a photo if it's too bright.
- Shadows and blacks, lighten and darken just the dark parts of the image. Eg you could lighten up the shadows of a photo.

Crop a Photo

To crop a photo, click on it in the photos section. Then click the adjustments icon on the top right.

Select the icon on the top right of the panel on the right hand side of the photo.

You'll see the photo open up in a grid. On each corner of the grid, you'll see a resize handle. To crop the image, click and drag these handles around the part of the image you want to keep.

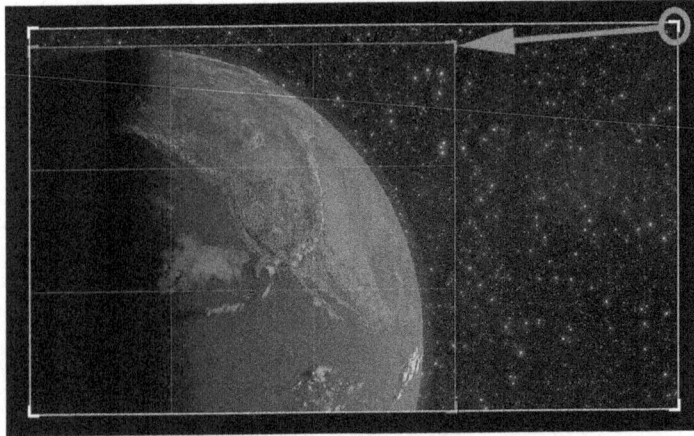

Click 'done' to accept the changes.

Rotate Photos

To rotate an image, use the slider on the right hand side. Click where it says 0° then drag up or down until the image is level.

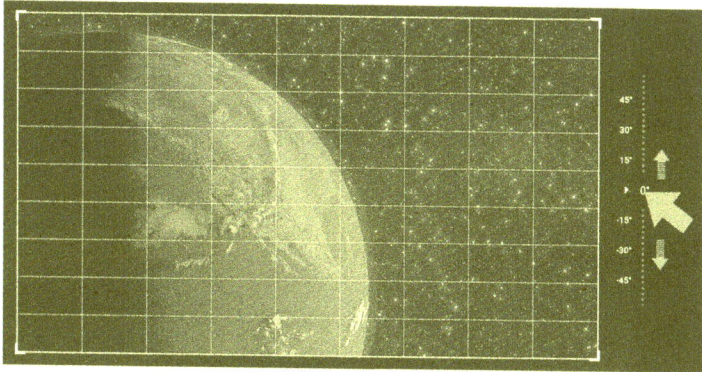

You can also rotate the image 90° counter clockwise using the icon on the top right.

To crop to an aspect ratio of the image, eg 16:8 or 4:3, click the aspect ratio icon on the top right.

Click 'done' on the top of the screen, when you're finished. Click the arrow on the left to return to your photos.

Creating Photo Albums

Select the photos you want to add to your album.

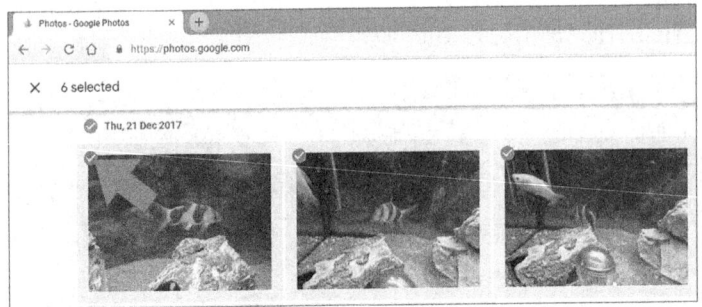

From the panel across the top of the screen, click the 'create' icon on the right hand side.

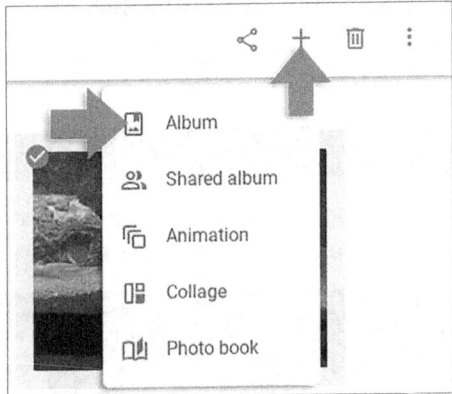

Click 'new album' to create a new album.

Give your album a name, then click the blue 'tick' icon on the top left of the screen.

You'll find all your albums in your 'album' section of Google Photos. Select 'albums' from the panel on the left hand side of the screen.

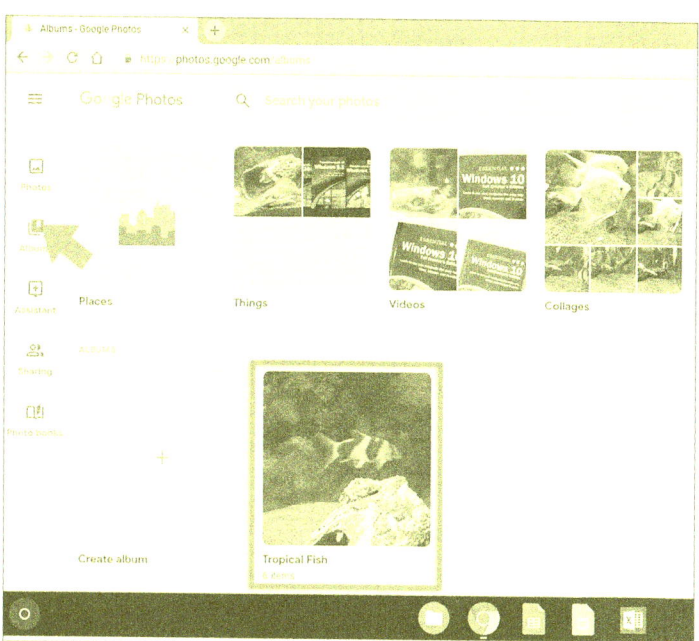

Creating Photo Collages

A photo collage is a composition made up of various different photographs assembled together. These are useful for posting to social media. To create a collage, select the photos you want to use from an album or the photos section. Choose six good ones.

Click the 'create' icon on the top right of the screen. From the drop down menu select 'collage'.

Click the adjustments icon to add a filter, or adjust the colour and brightness.

Click the share icon at the top to post your collage to social media, or send to a friend using email.

You'll find all collages you have created in your albums section.

Sharing Photos

Select the photo(s) you want to share from the photos section in Google Photos.

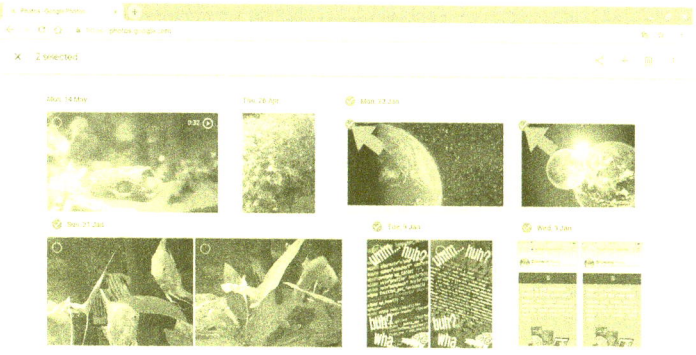

Click the 'share' icon on the top right of the screen.

Select the people you want to share the photos with.

Type in a message if you want to, then click the send icon.

When the other people check their email, they'll receive a message inviting them to view the photographs you shared.

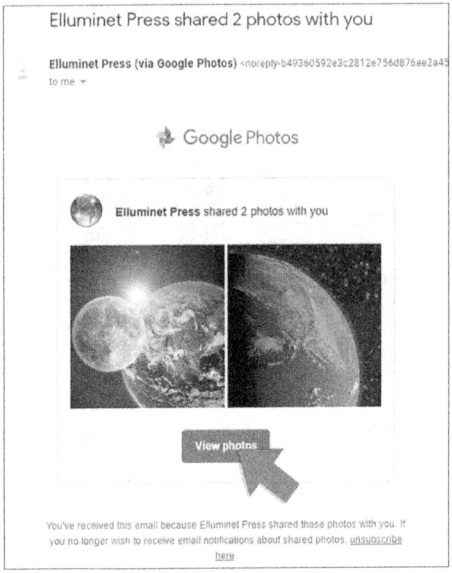

Click 'view photos' to open them up in Google Photos.

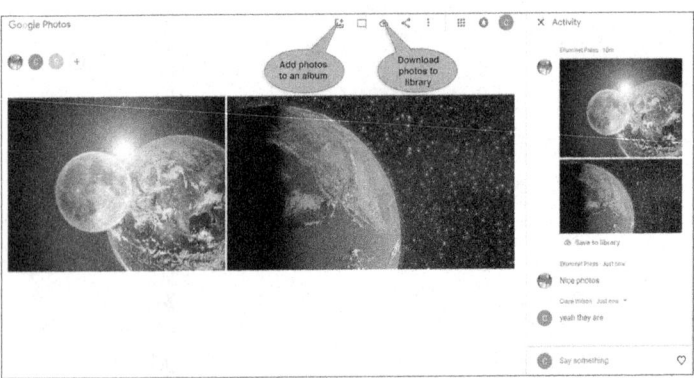

The person you shared your photos with can download them to their library, as well as add comments, and re share them with other people.

Power Up

To power up your ChromeBook, press the power key on the top right hand side of the keyboard. The Chrome logo will appear on the screen while the system starts.

Power Off

To shut down your ChromeBook, hold the power button for 1 second, you'll see three options pop up onto the screen.

Click 'power off' to shut down your ChromeBook. Click 'sign out' to sign out of your account and return to the login screen. Click 'lock screen' to lock your screen - useful if you are working on something and need to quickly lock your screen if you need to leave your ChromeBook for a few minutes without having to sign out completely.

If your ChromeBook has frozen or crashed, hold the power key until the screen goes blank. Wait a few seconds, then press the power key again to start up your ChromeBook

Enable Android Apps

Some Chromebooks don't support android apps, but most of the newer Chromebooks do. You'll need to enable the feature. To do this, open settings.

In the 'Google Play Store' section, turn on 'Install apps and games from Google Play on your Chromebook'.

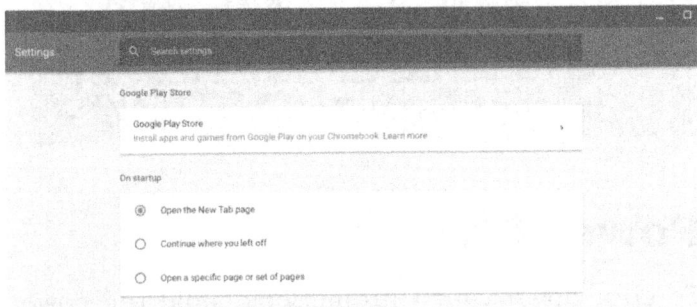

Note: If you don't see this option, your Chromebook doesn't support Android apps.

Install Android Apps

To install Android apps, open the Google Play Store on your app launcher. Or go to

play.google.com/store/apps

Search or browse for and app.

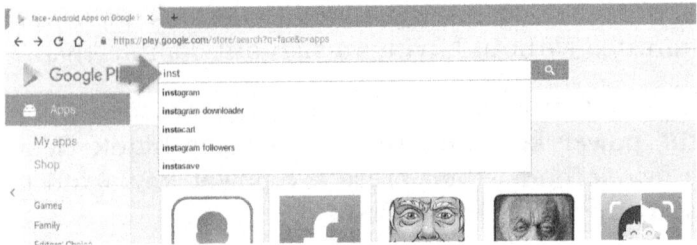

Click on the app to see more details.

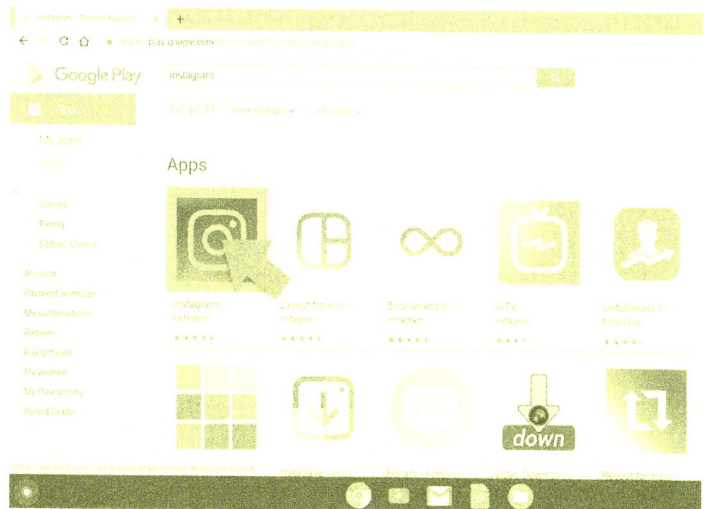

Click 'Install' (for free items) or the item's price to begin the installation.

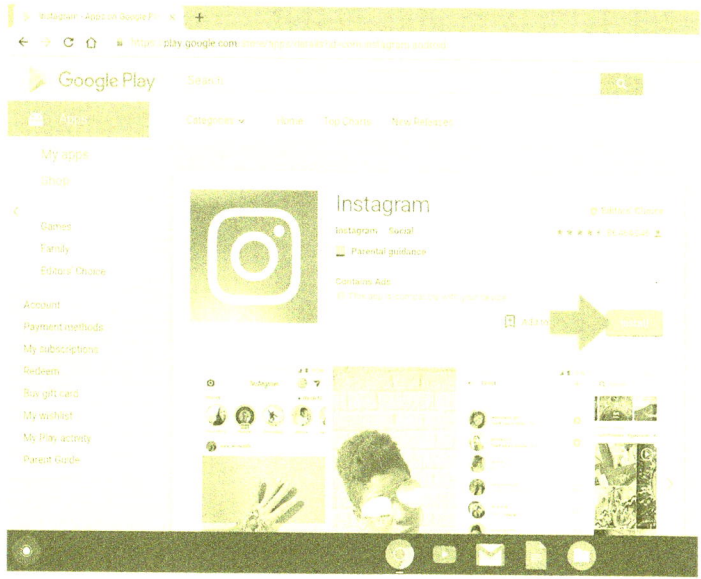

You'll find the app on your launcher.

Minimise an App

To quickly minimise an open app, press Alt minus.

Press that same key sequence again to bring the app or window back up into its previous position.

Maximise an App

To quickly minimise an open app, press Alt plus.

Press that same key sequence again to bring the app or window back up into its previous position.

Flick Between Open Apps

To flick between open apps, hold down Alt, and tap tab each time to flick between the apps.

Screen Brightness

Use the adjustment keys on the top of your keyboard

Volume Control

Use the adjustment keys on the top of your keyboard

Mute All

Press the mute button to mute all audio.

Autohide Shelf

You can hide the shelf when you're running apps to make use of the full screen. Right click on the launcher icon on the bottom left.

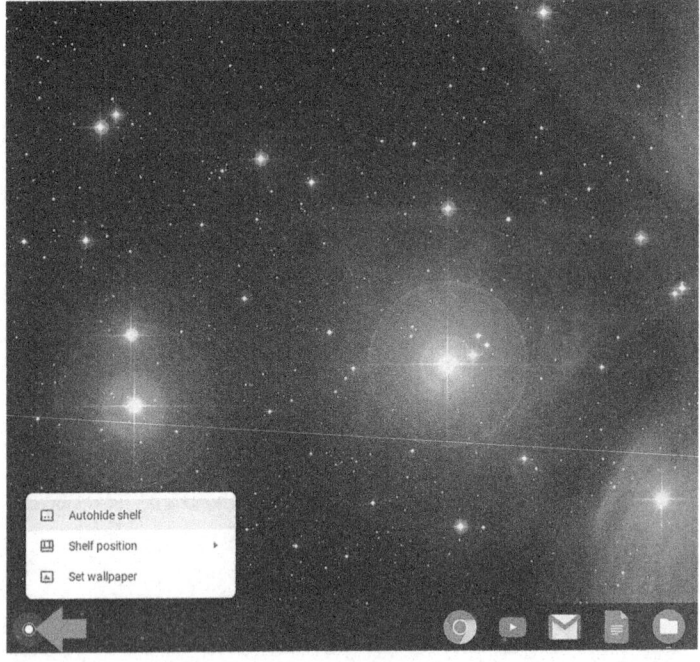

Select 'autohide shelf'. Now the shelf will disappear. To bring it back, move your mouse pointer to the bottom of the screen.

Zoom into your Screen

You can make the screen appear bigger by zooming in.

To zoom in press Ctrl Shift +.

Zoom out of your Screen

You can make the screen appear smaller by zooming out.

To zoom out press Ctrl Shift -

Reset Screen Zoom

To reset the zoom level press Ctrl Shift 0

Index

A

Add Event 58
Adding Users 28
Albums 94
All Open Apps 13
Android Apps 100
App Folders 19
App Launcher 17
App Shelf 9
Autohide Shelf 104

B

Bluetooth 26
Bluetooth Devices 26
Bookmarking Websites 47
Brightness 103

C

Calendar 58
Chrome Apps 70
ChromeCast 77, 83
Cloud Print 22
Collages 96
Contact from Message , 57
Contrast 91
Crop 92

D

Delete Apps 20
Delete Key 15
Desktop 9
Display All Open Apps 13
Documents 36

Drag , 12
DropBox 63

E

eBooks 86
Email 51
Email Accounts 55
Email Attachments 52
End Key 16
Exposure 91
External Drives 31

F

Factory Reset 68
Family Plan 76
Flash Drive 31

G

Google Assistant 8
Google Cloud Print 22
Google Docs 36
Google Drive 42
Google Sheets 38
Google Slides 40
Google Voice Assistant 8
Guest 33

H

Hangouts 61
Highlights 91
Home Key 16

K

Keyboard Shortcuts 14

L

Launching Apps 17
Lock Your Screen 32

M

Maximise an App 102
Minimise an App 102
Movies 78
Music 73
Mute 104

O

Offline 45
OK Google 8
OneDrive 64
Other Users 28

P

Pairing Devices 26
Photo Albums 94
Photo Collages 96
Photo Enhancements 90
Photo Filters 90
Photos 89
Pin Apps , 18
Pin Websites to your Shelf 50
Power Off 99
Power Up , 99
Powerwash 68
Preferences 10
Presentations 40
Printers 22
Printing Webpages 49

R

Remote Desktop 65
Remove Apps 20
Right Click 11
Rotate 93

S

Screen Brightness 103
Screenshots 33
Scroll , 12
SD Card 30
Settings 10
Shadows 91
Sharing Photos 97
shelf 9
Shutdown 99
Spreadsheets 38
Streaming 76
Streaming Music 76
Swipe , 13

T

Tap , 11
Task Manager 21
Transferring Files 46
TV Programs 84

U

Uninstall Apps 20
Updating ChromeOS 69
Users 28

V

Volume Control 103

W

Wallpaper , 34
Working Offline 45

Y

Youtube 85

Z

Zoom in 105
Zoom out 105

Made in the USA
Monee, IL
07 February 2020